Noah Webster

Effects of slavery on morals and industry.

Noah Webster

Effects of slavery on morals and industry.

ISBN/EAN: 9783743377028

Manufactured in Europe, USA, Canada, Australia, Japa

Cover: Foto ©ninafisch / pixelio.de

Manufactured and distributed by brebook publishing software
(www.brebook.com)

Noah Webster

Effects of slavery on morals and industry.

EFFECTS

OF

SLAVERY,

ON

MORALS AND INDUSTRY.

~~~~~~~~~~~~~~~~~~~~~~~~~

By NOAH WEBSTER, Jun. Efq.

Counfellor at Law and Member of the Connecticut Society for the
Promotion of Freedom.

~~~~~~~~~~~~~~~~~~~~~~~~~

The Gods are juft, and of our pleafant vices
Make inftruments to fcourge us.

SHAKESPEAR.

~~~~~~~~~~~~~~~~~~~~~~~~~

HARTFORD, (CONNECTICUT)
PRINTED BY HUDSON AND GOODWIN,
M,DCC,XCIII.

To

The *Connecticut Society for the Promotion of Freedom and the Relief of Persons unlawfully holden in Bondage,* This small Treatise, designed to exhibit some pernicious effects of Slavery, on the moral character, the industry and prosperity of nations, is most respectfully inscribed, by their most obedient and humble servant,

The AUTHOR.

ADVERTISEMENT.

I have for several years past had it in contemplation to write and publish some remarks on the pernicious conse-quences of slavery. Being appointed, by the society for the promotion of freedom, to deliver the annual Oration at Hartford, in May 1793, I took this opportunity of throw-ing together a few thoughts on the subject contemplated, and finding that the compass of an Oration would not be sufficient to admit even the general ideas and facts which, it was apprehended, might be necessary to illustrate the subject, I have chosen to publish the following remarks in the form of an essay or small treatise, and address it to the society, as a tribute of gratitude for the respect paid me, and as the best service I could render to the institution.

The views of slavery here exhibited, if not novel, are certainly important; and more time and materials than I can now command, are necessary to give them their due consideration.

HARTFORD, *May* 9. 1793.

EFFECTS of SLAVERY, &c.

THE injuftice of enflaving any part of the human race has been the fubject of fo much public difcuffion, and is fo generally admitted by the inhabitants of Connecticut, that any attempt to prove it, would be a very ill compliment to the underftandings of my enlightened fellow citizens. Nor could any efforts of mine add novelty to the fubject ; fo numerous, elaborate and diffufe have been the effays, and fo powerful the eloquence employed in vindicating the violated rights of humanity, that language and rhetoric are exhaufted.

But men, inftructed by their avarice in a fpecies of fubtle cafuiftry, have learnt to make a material diftinction between *abftract rights* and *private intereft or policy.* In defending the African Slave trade, its advocates, compelled by the powers of reafon to abandon the *right,* have taken refuge under the *policy* and *neceffity* of the traffic. Here entrenched as in a ftrong hold, they maintain their ftation, and bid defiance to the attacks of reafon and religion. To drive them from this citadel of defence, it becomes neceffary to encounter them with their own weapons, and upon their own ground.

As the only fteady, permanent and uniform fpring of men's actions, is a regard to their fuppofed intereft, if we would effectually reftrain them from the purfuit of any object, we muft firft convince them that the object, if obtained, will not produce them the real benefit and happinefs which they expect. It is not fufficient to perfuade nations concerned in the flave trade, that the practice of enflaving their brethren of the human race, is barbarous and wicked, and that it is a violation of the laws of nature and fociety. Previous to their relinquifhing the practice, they muft be convinced that fuch relinquifhment will not be materially prejudicial to their intereft.

To endeavor to prove this important truth, that *flavery,* in all its forms and varieties, is repugnant to the private intereft and public happinefs of man, is the tafk I have affigned myfelf in this effay though neither my talents nor my opportunities of acquiring the; neceffary information, will enable me to do juftice to the fubject.

In taking this comprehensive view of the effects of slavery on men and nations, the society, to whom this treatise is addressed, will pardon me, if I do not restrict myself to the consideration of the African slave trade and the more immediate purposes of their institution; for the effects of despotism and a violent restraint of the natural liberty of man, are the same in all countries; subject however to inconsiderable modifications from climate, soil, religion, or other incidental circumstances.

SLAVERY may be divided into, *political* and *civil. Political slavery,* is a subjection to the uncontrolled exercise of public authority, whether that authority is in the hands of a king, a council, or a popular assembly. *Civil slavery* is a subjection to the absolute power of a particular proprietor, or master.

SLAVERY also exists in very different degrees in different countries. In some countries, the slave possesses by custom, or enjoys by indulgence, some rights and privileges; in others, he is stripped of all rights, and his services, his person and his life, are at the arbitrary disposal of his master. But as I am not about forming a systematic treatise on this subject, these distinctions will not be pursued; it being sufficient for my purpose to exhibit the *general effects of slavery on men and nations.*

OF the effects of slavery, the first in order are those which respect the *character of the slave;* indeed most of the pernicious consequences of slavery, whether public or private, may be traced to this one source, the *effects of an unnatural and an unwarrantable restraint laid upon the will of the slave.*

IT is evidently the will of heaven that men should be prompted to action by a regard to their own benefit and happiness. Whenever by the positive institutions of society, or by external force, men are stripped of the power of exerting themselves for their own benefit, the mind, having lost its spring or stimulus, either ceases to act, and men become mere machines, moving only when impelled by some extraneous power; or if the mind acts at all, it is at the impulse of violent passions, struggling to throw off an unnatural restraint, and to revenge the injury. Hence it is, that slaves, with few exceptions, may be divided into two classes, the *indolent* and the *villanous.*

IN America the laziness of slaves has become proverbial: indeed the blacks are so remarkable for their inaction, their want of foresight and their disinclination to improvement, as to create very great doubts in the minds of some men of a philosophical cast, whether they are not a distinct and inferior race of beings.† But on examining this subject, and comparing the blacks of this country, with the slaves of other countries, who are confessedly of the same race with the most improved European nation, it will probably be found that, making the usual allowances for the effects of their native climate, all the peculiar features in the character of the African race in America, may justly be ascribed to their depressed condition.

† See Hume's Essays vol. 1. p. 550. Note. M. Jefferson's notes on Virginia, p. 297.

The indolence of the slaves in the southern states, must indeed approach almost to stupidity. It is said by gentlemen, well informed on this subject, that three blacks will not perform more labor than one free white in the northern states.[*] And it is well known that on every plantation, a negro driver is required, with his whip and his cane, to compel the reluctant slave to perform his daily task. But are American slaves only distinguished for their aversion to labor? History teaches us a very different doctrine. Among the antient Germans, who, by their vigor and bravery, conquered half the world, slavery had the same debasing stupifying influence; and it is remarkable that the word *lazzi*, which among our Saxon ancestors, was the denomination or the lowest order of bondmen or servants, is the origin of our English word *lazy*, a word expressive of that indolence and aversion to labor, which remarkably characterize the negroes in America.[†] If slavery had this effect upon our own ancestors, the warlike heroes of the *north*, surely modern philosophers need not resort to an original difference of race, for the cause of that dullness and want of mental vigor, remarkable in the enslaved natives of the *torrid zone* and their degenerate descendants.

But if we turn our eyes upon the present nations of Europe, we shall find multiplied proofs of this important truth, that slavery necessarily enervates the vigor of the human mind, in all climates and among all nations.

In Poland, the peasants, who are slaves, are so indolent that they do not furnish themselves even with a shelter from the inclemencies of the weather. The proprietor of the land to which the peasants are annexed, like the stock of a farm, is obliged to build cottages and barns for them, and to furnish them with seed, plows, horses, and every implement of husbandry.[§] Nor do these miserable wretches provide themselves the ordinary comforts of life. Little more is to be seen within their hovels, than bare walls, a wooden stool, and a bed of straw. People who travel in that desolate country, and expect tolerable accommodations, must carry with them their own beds, their provisions, their knives, forks and spoons.[‡]

Very little better is the condition of the peasantry throughout the immense Russian empire.[||] So abject is their situation and so complete the degradation of their minds, as to give rise to a general opinion in that country, that the peasants, if set at liberty, would not be capable of procuring a subsistence.[¶]

The modern inhabitants of Greece, are remarkable for their aversion to active employments. The miserable subjects of the Turk-

* MSS. letter from the hon. Dr. Ramsay, of Charlestown South-Carolina.
† From the same root have sprung the words *lazaretto* and *lazzaroni*, in the Italian language, the latter of which is the general name given to the idlers and beggars that swarm in Italy; and the former, is the name of the hospitals erected for the sick and infirm among those miserable wretches. See Moor's Italy and Brydone's tour, passim.
§ Coxe's travels into Poland, &c. vol. 1. p. 160.
‡ Ibm. page 251. || Ibm. p. 890.
¶ Ibm. vol. 2. 246.

ish government pass whole days, musing, with their legs crossed, their pipes in their mouths, and almost without changing their attitude. Athens and Sparta, the fields of Marathon, Platea, and Thermopylæ, those nurses of heroes, lawgivers and philosophers, or the theaters on which they exercised their talents and displayed atchievements, that still excite astonishment, are now inhabited by lazy Turks and a few Greeks, dispirited and debased, who inherit not one of the virtues of their illustrious ancestors. To what cause shall we attribute this degeneracy of the Greeks? To what physical energy? Surely no change of climate, no alteration in the productive powers of nature, can account for this moral phenomenon. To despotism alone, that foul monster, before whose pestilential breath, the powers of the mind wither and decay, must we ascribe this woful debasement of the modern Greeks.

ANOTHER effect of slavery upon its miserable subjects is to make them *cruel, deceitful, perfidious*, and *knavish*; in short, to deprive them of all the noble and amiable affections of the human heart. This fatal and necessary consequence of oppression upon the moral character of man, though often noticed by the historian, the divine and philosopher, has either escaped the reflection of tyrants, or its admonitions have been hushed by the more commanding calls of a mistaken selfish policy. But proofs of this truth are scattered over almost every page of history. We can scarely open a volume without finding some fact to convince us that *oppression is the mother of crimes*. So striking was this truth in antient Greece, that a great philosopher† doubted, whether there was any one virtue belonging to slaves. How can it be otherwise? Is it expectable that men, who are precluded by violence from enjoying the *benefits* of society, should cultivate the *virtues* from which its blessings flow? Is it not more natural that the subjects of oppression, sensible they are robbed of their rights and resenting the injury, should perpetually struggle to indemnify themselves for the loss, and when it would be fruitless to use open force, that they should have recourse to the arts of treachery and fraud? The principles of human nature warrant this conclusion, and account for the detestable character of slaves in all ages and all countries.

The Moors in Algiers and Morocco, are generally given to robbery and piracy; and people cannot travel in safety at a distance from the towns in their country, without a marabout or reputed saint, for a guard. The Turks in the same countries have not the same character. Why this difference? Has nature impressed their different characters? A more satisfactory answer is, that the Moors, considering themselves the original proprietors of the countries, and by the conquest of the Turks, reduced to a state of poverty and

---

* Volney's travels, vol. 2. 461. It must be remarked that the blacks, who, in America, will scarcely move without a negro driver at their heels, are, in their own conntry, a very gay lively people. Abr. of Buffon's works, p. 64.

† Aristotle, polit, lib. 1.

difgrace, unable, at the fame time, to throw off the yoke of bondage, betake themfelves to theft and robbery, and plunder all *they meet by way of reprifal.*

THE Malayan flaves in the Dutch plantations at the Cape of Good Hope, are very intelligent, but attrocious villains. To affaffinate their mafters is a common crime; and the culprit, who has committed it, marches to the fcaffold with an air of unconcern; or rejoices that he has taken a ftep which will put an end to his life and his fervitude. ||

THE Mamlouks of Egypt, a band of military flaves, firft formed out of the prifoners which Genghis Khan took in his famous expedition into Perfia and the countries on the borders of the Cafpian Sea A D 1227, have ever been diftinguifhed for their turbulent fpirit, their perfidy, and ferocious cruelty. Like the Prætorian bands of the Roman Emperors, and the Janizaries of Turkey, they depofed their chiefs at pleafure, and in the 257 years, when Egypt was fubject to their military defpotifm, forty feven of their leaders fell by the fword or by poifon ; by public murder or private affaffination. †

THE Greeks under the Turkifh government are theivifh, deceitful, treacherous, and mean even to a proverb : abject in adverfity and infolent in profperity.¶ Even their features are vifibly diftorted with knavery and meannefs, and the traveller reads, in their crouching looks, that they are flaves.‡

IN ancient Rome, when a mafter was murdered, all his flaves under the fame roof or within the hearing of a man's voice, were by law condemned to death.§ Was not this inhuman law founded on the prefumption that flaves were prone to commit crimes of this attrocious nature, and that they were all principals or acceffories? that they were fo abandoned and unprincipled in the opinion of a Roman Senate as not to be deferving of a legal procefs and conviction? The feverity of laws is always preceded by a corruption of manners, and in a free ftate, it is the criterion by which we may afcertain the degree of national depravity. Permit me to remark further that in the opinion and the laws of the Romans, *theft* was confidered moft exclufively the *crime of flaves.***

BUT there is not a more demonftrative evidence of the direct tendency of flavery to deprave and vitiate the heart, than the change in the fignification of the words *villain* and *knave. Villain,* in ancient times, fignified a bondman or tenant who was annexed

---

* Encyclopedia vol. 1. p. 454.
|| Vaillant's Travels Vol. 1. p. 56.
† Volneys Travels Vol. 1. p. 193, 104.
¶ Volney's Travels a vol. 489. Savary's Letter on Greece p. 141.
‡ Ibm. p. 308. 309. § Montfq. B. 15. ch. 15. Tac. An. lib. 14. ca. 42.
** De Lolme on the Conftit. of Engl. p. 113 N Y Edit. Tacitus An. lib. 14 ca. 43 fays exprefsly, " fufpecta majoribus noftris fuere ingenia fervorum, etiam cum in agris aut domibus iifdem" nafcerentur caritatemque dominorum ftatim acciperent.

to the foil as a cultivator of the earth and bound to perform fervile offices.* *Knave*, in the primitive Saxon, fignified a *male child* or *boy*, and as boys were much ufed for *domeftic fervants*, it came afterward to denote any *man fervant*.‡ From this circumftance alone, *the pronenefs of men in a degraded-fphere of life to contract vicious habits*, it has happened that thefe words, *villain* and *knave*, have loft their ancient fignification, and become almoft the appropriate names of perfons addicted to fraud and deceit or guilty of enormous crimes. The words anciently conveyed no idea of difhonefty, more than *bondman* and *fervant* do now ; and the complete transfer of their fignification from the deftination of the *perfons*, to their *properties*, is a decifive proof that the qualities which take the names, are predominant characteriftic qualities of thofe denominations of men. In fhort, it is a fingular and ftriking evidence that flaves have always been, as we now fee them to be, prone to commit petty knaviſh tricks or grofs villanies.

Why does Ireland abound with thieves and robbers ? are its natives more depraved by nature than the natives of other countries? This will not be afferted ; for the honour, integrity and liberality which diftinguifh Hibernians of property and education, overthrow all fuch theories. But oppreffion, with her iron fcepter, rules that devoted country. The peafants, fubject to the combined operation of civil and political flavery, are fenfible they are ftripped of their natural and focial rights ; without property or reputation to lofe ; without the hope of making their condition better or the fear of making it worfe, the ragged victims of avarice and oppreffion lurk about the large towns, prepared for clandeftine plunder, or with the ferocious fpirit of defperadoes, ftalk along the highways and boldly rob the defencelefs paffenger. But let the poor of Ireland be raifed to the condition of freeholders, let them have property and enjoy the fruits of their induftry, let their children be educated to honeft employments, and Tyburn would no longer be thronged with the wretched natives of that infulted country, nor would the Iflands of the Pacific Ocean be annually peopled with frefh fupplies of Irifh Convicts.

THE character of the Jews is another proof of the doctrine here advanced. Tho never fubject to domeftic and civil flavery, like the Africans in America, yet from the time of their difperfion, they have fuffered innumerable hardfhips and injuries from the prejudices of chriftian princes and a biggoted clergy. † Confidered as infidels and outcafts on earth, they have been deprived of the privi-

---

* Fleta. lib. 4. chap. 2. Glanvill. lib. 5. cap. 1. Coke upon Lit. 117.
‡ Cowel. in verbum.
† The Jews were rendered incapable of holding lands in England in the reign of Edward I. AD 1275. Multitudes were executed in 1278 on fufpicion of clipping the coin ; and banifhed the kingdom for their ufury and their religion in 1290. Smollet. Hift. Eng. vol. 2. 254. 258. 273.
In France, they were abandoned, on fufpicion or frivolous pretences, to the plunder of the populace, about the year 1321. Hift. of France vol. 2 240. At this day Jews are not permitted to refide in Ruffia. Coxe.

lege of holding lands in some countries, * in others subjected to unreasonable taxes and rigorous restraints and not unfrequently exposed to persecution. Thus treated wherever they were dispersed, and being never secure of a peaceable residence of any considerable duration, they rarely or never betook themselves to agriculture or mechanical employments ; but vested their property in moveables, which could be easily concealed or conveyed from place to place, and more especially in money. From this circumstance, it happened that Jews in the infancy of commerce became the brokers of all Europe, and compelled by necessity to turn their whole attention to money-transactions, they very early reduced them to a science. By this means they commanded almost all the money of the countries where they were settled in numbers, and partly thro their precarious situation, and partly thro the necessities of other people, they every where had recourse to the practice of lending money at an exorbitant interest. This increased the popular odium which was before entertained against this race of unbelievers, and in some countries, it rose so high as to occasion their banishment. But their occupations and the modes of business which they have been compelled to *pursue* by the jealousy which has hunted them in almost every part of Christendom, have given them the reputation of *Sharpers* ; and it is not supposeable that the general opprobrium they suffer is totally without foundation. If in modern times, the Jews have ceased to deserve this odious epithet, as I presume, in many countries, they have, the change is to be attributed to a more liberal policy in government ; and if the time has not yet arrived, it will soon arrive at least in America and France, when Jews, admitted to the equal rights of other citizens, will wipe away the reproach from their national character.

ANOTHER fact to prove how generally mankind admit the tendency of slavery to corrupt the human heart, and how little they have been hitherto influenced by the important truth, is the exclusion of a slave's testimony from trials at Law.

By the laws of ancient Rome, slaves could not be admitted as witnesses, and Montesquieu approves of the exclusion.‖ Under the Emperor Augustus a law was made to enfranchise slaves for the purpose of rendering them admissible witnesses in cases of high Treason ; but by an edict of the Emperor Tacitus, this law was abrogated.

By the laws of Poland, the testimony of the peasants, tho not excluded from courts, is considered as of less weight than that of freemen. If a lord kills his slave, the murder must be proved by *two* Gentlemen or *four* peasants ; the testimony of *two* freemen being deemed equivalent to that of *four* slaves.‡

IN this state, slaves are admitted as witnesses at the discretion

* Poland is almost the only country in Europe where the Jews cultivate the earth. Here they enjoy extensive privileges and are very industrious useful citizens. Coxe vol. 1. 170. 163.
‖ Book 12. Ch. 15.   ‡ Coxe's travels into Poland, &c. vol. 1, p. 158

of the Court ; but in some of the southern States it is never thot proper to resort to their testimony.†

THE natural enquiry is why a slave should be a less credible witness than a freeman. The answer is easy ; *slavery corrupts the heart.* Exceptions to this rule may be found ; but the laws or the practice of most nations warrants the assertion, that slaves have generally been considered as less influenced by a sense of honor and by moral obligations than freemen.* Of this fact there can be no doubt ; and it is a curious inconsistency in legislation, that laws should be made, enjoining moral and religious duties and prohibiting almost every species of vice, yet indirectly or expressly countenancing the practice of enslaving men, which, in the first instance, is the most attrocious act of villany, and in its consequences, destructive of all sense of moral obligation and introductive of every species of crimes.

It is a striking illustration of these ideas, that countries where the oppressions of the feudal system and domestic slavery still exist, are much more infested with pilferers and robbers, than free republican states, where the citizens are freeholders and not generally proprietors of slaves. In Great Britain, Ireland, Spain, Italy, most parts of Germany, and throughout the immense Turkish and Russian territories, the traveller must go armed and watch his baggage with continual assiduity for fear of highwaymen, and pickpockets. In the free Swifs Cantons,‡ and in Sweden,‡ such precautions are hardly necessary ; and in the northern States of America where there are few slaves, and those resident mostly in the large towns, a man may travel month after month, alone and unarmed, and except on the great roads and in the vicinity of the populous towns, he may leave his baggage on his horse or in his carriage in the open highway, with great safety, or even in the bar-room of a public inn. Except in or near the great towns, scarcely a robbery has been committed, and most of the few offenders in this way, have been foreigners, who had become villains at home, and had fled or been transported for their crimes.

THIS doctrine respecting the influence of slavery is verified by the general character of the negroes in the United States of America. The natives of Africa, who are introduced into the West Indies and these States, are of different tribes, and considerably different in respect to particular traits of character. But in general we may observe with Mon. Buffon,‖ that the Negroes of Africa, are a remarkably innocent and inoffensive people. If properly fed and well treated, they are contented, joyous and obliging ; if exposed to harsh brutal treatment, their spirits forsake them, and they droop with sorrow. Alike impressed with a sense of the injuries they suffer, and the favours they receive, to a cruel master, they are impla-

---

† Jefferson Notes. p. 237. * See the note in page 9 from Tacitus.
‡ Coxe's Switz. vol. 1 223 and both volumes, passim. Coxe's Russia and Sweden vol. 1. 305. iii. 85. See Born's Travels. 10. 42.
‖ Abridgement of his works. p. 64.

caple foes ; to an indulgent one, faithful and affectionate servants.
I am not personally acquainted with any slaves in Connecticut, who
were born in Africa, and who arrived to manhood in their own
country, before they were reduced to bondage. I have therefore had
no opportunity to observe what general difference exists between
the moral character of an African, enslaved after he had grown, to
years of manhood, and that of a black who was born and bred in
slavery. On general principles, it is to be presumed, that Africans,
who are bred in freedom, and enslaved after they have acquired habits of frankness and ingenuousness of deportment, will either re-
tain through life a large portion of their early virtues ; and if they
attempt to redress their own wrongs, that they will be bold and man-
ly in their attacks upon their oppressors. Negroes, on the other
hand, who are born and nursed under the pressure of bondage, will
be destitute of that openness of character which marks the wild freedom of savages, and their minds will sink into a state of sullen apa-
thy ; or prompted to action by a sense of injury and restrained by
fear from open violence, they will exercise their ingenuity in devi-
sing and committing petty frauds on their masters. However this
may be, it is a known fact that the blacks in this country, are, with
few exceptions, addicted to the practice of committing little clan-
destine frauds, and a large proportion of capital crimes, will on ex-
amination, be found to be perpetrated by the same race of men.
Not a year passes, but we hear of the burglaries, the rapes, or the
murders committed by the blacks in the United States,† Nor does
the restoration of freedom in general correct the depravity of their
hearts. Born and bred beneath the frowns of power, neglected and
despised in youth, they abandon themselves to ill company and low
vicious pleasures, till their habits are formed ; when manumission,
instead of destroying their habits and repressing their corrupt incli-
nations, serves to afford them more numerous opportunities of in-
dulging both. Thus an act of strict justice to the slave very often
renders him a worse member of society. This idea is not suggested
as an argument against the liberation of slaves from the yoke of
bondage ; but it proves very fully, that a bare emancipation of them
is not an act of adequate justice, much less is it *all* that good citizens *may* do towards correcting their ill habits and rendering them
valuable members of the community.

THE general character of the slaves in the West-Indies corres-
ponds with the description here given of the blacks in the United
States. They are stubborn and untractable, and the perverseness of
their dispositions is alledged by the planters as an excuse for the
severe and harsh discipline exercised over these unhappy people.
But when the negroes first arrive from the coast of Africa, they are
simple and inoffensive men ; and when, after being some time dril-

---

† Two or three instances of murder committed by slaves on their masters,
happened in Virginia the last year. The same crime is frequent in the
West-Indies. In the northern states where there are few slaves and those
treated with more lenity, they seldom murder the whites, but they are much
addicted to stealing, and often commit burglary.

led to service by their drivers, they remain dull or turn arrant knaves, and are punished for their crimes and laziness, they justify themselves by the example of the whites.*

From the universal depravity of slaves, from a keen sense of the injuries they suffer and a strong desire of revenge, have sprung numerous insurrections, which have frequently deluged whole countries in blood. Hardened by severe labor, exasperated at insults, disciplined in cruelty, and armed with dispair, they become doubly ferocious ; and their insurrections are marked with more than savage barbarity. The passions of men resemble the current of a majestic river, which while it meets with no resistance, glides smoothly on, silent and harmless ; attacked with boisterous winds, it moves with sullen dignity, heaving its murmuring waves against the re founding shores ; but when massy mounds impede its progress, it rises in all its force, and bursting its banks with indignant fury, it spreads wide havoc and devastation over the adjacent plains—Such have been the ravages committed by slaves, when, unable any longer to bear the pressure of their bondage, despair has roused their spirit to burst their fers asunder, and they have risen in myriads to avenge their wrongs.

A history of the calamities and dangers which nations have suffered by the revolt of their slaves, would teach us a most useful lesson ; but the recital in detail would fill the mind with horror, A few instances only will be here added to the black catalogue of public and private evils flowing from the practice of enslaving men which this essay is intended to exhibit.

In the year of Rome 293, during the Consulship of C. Claudius, and P. Valerius Publicola, about 4000 slaves and exiles, headed by Ap. Herdonius, a sabine of a bold ambitious character, entered the city by night, and seized the capitol, with the temple of Jupiter. From this fortress, they made excursions and with merciless fury, butchered all the citizens they found, who refused to join the conspiracy. An alarm was soon spread thro the city ; the danger was magnified by the darkness of the night, and the Romans not knowing who were their enemies, nor what their force, were filled with consternation. Day light at length disclosed the author and nature of the commotion : and Rome, distracted with the violent contests between the Patricians and Plebeians, expected a general insurrection of slaves and desperadoes within its own walls.† The consuls, by a vigorous exertion of their power and by liberal promises to the plebeians, persuaded the people to take arms and rescue the capitol from their foes ; but one of the consuls and a

---

* Guth. Geog. p. 832. Clarkson's Essay on the slavery and commerce of the human species. page 105.
† Hooke's Rom Hist. vol 1. 286. Liv. lib 3. c. 15. 16. Livy gives a concise, but lively description of the suspicion and terror excited by this insurrection of slaves ; a description often applicable to the situation of the planters in the West Indies. " Multi et varii timores ; inter ceteros eminebat terror servilis, ne suus cuique domi hostis esset. Cui nec credere, nec non credendo, ne infestior fieret, fidem abrogare, satis erat tutum."

multitude of citizens perished in the affault, and Rome was not, without difficulty, faved from a general Maffacre.

In the year 334, during the adminiftration of N. Fabius Vibulanus, and Quinctius Capitolinus, the flaves formed a confpiracy to fet fire to the City in various parts at once, and while the people fhould be engaged in extinguifhing the flames, they intended to take poffeffion of the tower and Capitol. Two of the confpirators revealed the plot and faved Rome from a civil war and the horrors of a conflagration.[†]

In the year of Rome 494, in the confulfhip of L. Cornelius Scipio and C. Aquilius Florus, a body of 3000 difcontented flaves, united with a number of Samnites, formed a defign to plunder and burn the city; but one of their leaders betrayed the plot and the confpiracy was fuppreffed.[‡]

In the year 556, under the confulate of T Quinctius Flamininus and Sextus Ælius Pœtus, the flaves who attended fome Carthaginian hoftages, who were perfons of diftinction, confpired together to feize the town of Setia, during the celebration of the games and flaughter the inhabitants. A timely difcovery, made by two flaves, prevented the execution of this nefarious defign.

Scarcely was the confpiracy fuppreffed in this quarter when a banditti of the fame flaves made an attempt to feize Præneftes; they were attacked by L. Cornelius the prætor and 500 of them put to the fword.[§]

Soon after Etruria, (the modern Tufcany,) was infefted with a revolt of flaves, which ended in the flaughter, captivity or crucifixion of the rebels.[*]

Not long after Apulia was difturbed with an infurrection of flaves, who infefted the roads with their robberies. Upon an enquiry before the Prætor, L. Poftumius, 7000 of them were condemned, of whom great numbers fled, and others fuffered the punifhment due to their crimes.[‖]

But thefe infurrections were petty mobs, compared with the fervile war in Sicily and Capua, which, on account of their refemblance to the revolt of the negroes in the Weft Indies, deferve a more particular defcription.

Sicily was the finest wheat country in the Roman dominions. Rome was fupplied from its granaries, and many of its cultivators became immenfely rich. Their wealth and pride led them to the practice of employing flaves in the cultivation of their farms, and towards the clofe of the Roman Republic, the flaves were multiplied to fuch a degree as to endanger the public fafety. The abufive treatment they received from their mafters, who fcarcely

---

† Liv. lib. 4. ca. 45. Hooke's Rom Hift. vol. 1. 389.
‡ Hooke. vol. 2. p. 28. It was the practice in Rome to reward the flaves, who informed the magiftrates of plots, with their freedom and large fums of money. See Livy in the paffages quoted.
§ Liv. lib. 32. ca. 26. * Liv. lib. 33. ca. 36.
‖ Liv. lib. 39. ca. 29.

allowed them food and raiment, drove them to feek fupport by rapine and plunder. At length the cruelty they fuffered excited an infurrection, and headed by one Eunus, an enthufiaft of their own number, they attacked the city of Enna and maffacred the inhabitants with indiferiminate fury. As they proceeded in ravaging the country, they were joined by other flaves, till they formed a body of *forty* thoufand men.*

From the year of Rome 615 to 621, the flaves were mafters of the Ifland ; they defeated the Roman armies under Manlius, Lentulus and Pifo, Prætors of Sicily; till at length the Conful Rupillius, by reftoring difcipline to their troops, obtained a victory over the infurgents, took their ftrong holds, flew 30,000 of their number and reftored peace to the Ifland. This example of the flaves in Sicily was followed by thofe in Italy and Greece, who made efforts to throw off the yoke of bondage. Thefe difturbances indeed were quelled without much difficulty or danger ; but the hiftorian Florus declares that Sicily was more cruelly wafted in the war with the flaves, than in the Carthaginian.†

In the year of Rome 680, Capua became the feat of a revolt. Spartacus, a heroic flave, being reduced to the condition of a gladiator and difdaining the infamous employment of fighting for the amufement of others, put himfelf at the head of the gladiators, and was foon joined by the flaves of the neighboring country. With an army of more than 70,000 defperadoes, he vanquifhed the Roman forces repeatedly and threatened Rome itfelf.

To quell this formidable infurrection, required all the ftrength of Rome ; and after numerous difafters, Craffus the Prætor routed Spartacus, deftroyed 60,000 of his men, fcattered the remainder and relieved Rome, then almoft miftrefs of the world, from the terror of her flaves. Five thoufand of the fugitives who were efcaping to the Alps, were met by Pompey, then returning victorious from Spain, and all put to the fword. Six thoufand fell alive into the hands of the Romans, and were crucified along the road from Capua to Rome.‡

It is remarked by Baron Montefquieu that, free ftates are much more liable to be convulfed by infurrections of flaves than defpotic governments. In free ftates, flaves fee others enjoying rights and happinefs of which they themfelves are deprived. They fee the lives and perfons of others guarded by laws, while their own are without protection. Their wretchednefs is aggravated by comparifon. In fuch ftates multitudes of flaves always prove dangerous to focie-

---

* Florus. lib. 3. ca. 19. Hooke. vol. 2. p. 540 fays their number was 200,000. I have followed Florus.

† Florus. lib. 3. ca. 19. The Romans confined great numbers of their flaves in cells or prifons, called *ergaftuls*, where they were chained to labor. The younger Pompey recruited his army from the *ergaftula* in Sicily and Sardinia. Florus. lib. 4. ca. 8.

‡ Florus. lib. 8. ca. 20. Liv. Epit. lib. 97. Hooke's Rom. Hift. vol. 3. 194 to 200.

ty.§ In despotic governments, where every man is little better than a slave, they are less to be dreaded, yet in these, severity may render them dangerous.

In the reign of John, King of France, about the middle of the 14th Century, and while that prince was a prisoner to Edward 3d of England, the peasants of France, oppressed by the nobility, harrassed by continual wars and exposed to the derision and contempt of their superiors, arose in myriads to avenge their wrongs and insults. With savage fury, they spread desolation over the kingdom; the castles of the nobles and gentry were burnt or levelled to the ground; their wives and daughters were violated or murdered; and the Lords who were taken prisoners by the barbarous herd, expired under the most exquisite torments. The nobles, at length associated and collected their forces to put an end to these horrid outrages. Ten thousand of the insurgents fell victims to the Duke of Orleans, in the neighborhood of Paris: the king of Navarre slew 12,000 more, with their principal leader, William Caillet; and 9000 others, who were besieging Meaux, were attacked with success and scattered or slain.‖

In the year 1525, the severe oppressions which the peasants of Franconia in Germany suffered from the nobility, roused them to open rebellion. The insurgents seized the princes and dukes, put collars about their necks, and loaded them with insults, crying out, " now we are masters and you are nothing."*

About 40 years ago, the Turkish slaves in the Island of Malta conspired to put an end to the whole order of knights. They had determined to poison all the fountains of water, and every slave had sworn to put his master to death. A most providential discovery prevented the execution of their design. The conspirators were seized; 125 were put to death, some being burnt alive, some broken on the wheel, and others torn to pieces by four galleys rowed different ways and each carrying off a limb. The 6th day of June, the anniversary of the discovery, is still celebrated by the order of Malta, as a day of Thanksgiving for their deliverance from this terrible conspiracy.†

The history of the European settlements in the West Indies abounds with facts which evince the perpetual danger to which men are exposed, when surrounded with slaves. The numerous insurrections of the negroes which have, at different times, harrassed those settlements, have taught the planters to depend on the bayonet only for the safety of their persons and estates. Nor will this resource always supply the want of confidence in the fidelity of their domestics. Treachery often eludes the watchman's eye, and the lordly *master* himself, tho surrounded with guards, becomes the *slave* of suspicion and distrust.

Without entering into a detail of the calamities and horrors

§ Montesq. vol. 1, 306.   Blacks com. vol. 1. 418.
‖ Hist. of France. vol. 1. page 275.
* Reisbeck's Travels vol, 2 294.   † Brydone's Tour. vol. 1. 227.

C

that have been occasioned in the West Indies by the attempts of slaves to recover their liberty and avenge their wrongs, it will be sufficient barely to mention the present deplorable state of the French colony in St. Domingo. The miseries of that Island are the theme of almost every gazette. To recapitulate them would be useless; for who among my readers does not recollect the accounts he has read the last two years? and whose blood is not chilled at recollecting the recitals of cruelty, outrage and murder which have marked the bloody scenes? Where is the civilized man, who has tasted the pleasures and known the value of peace and security, who can willingly renounce the enjoyment of both, for the sake of living in splendor, and yield himself a prey to the vexations of unceasing watchfulness and suspicion? Who can sacrifice the cheerfulness, contentment and confidence that reign among equals and fellow citizens, the felicities that bless a nation of freemen and freeholders, for the society of ignorant stupid slaves and treacherous dependants? Can the human mind be so debased as to rejoice in the wretchedness of man? Surely the master as well as the slave, must lose the sensibilities of his nature, and degenerate to a brute, before he can endure the sight of men doomed to linger out their existence in chains, bending beneath the pressure of heavy burthens, crippled with hard labor and bruises, emaciated with hunger, scourged by their merciless drivers, hopeless and forlorn, courting the relentless monster, *death*, to wrest them from the hands of that more unfeeling monster, *man*.*

This leads me to notice some effects of slavery on the character of the master. It is a general truth that the men who, from their infancy *hold*, and those who *feel*, the rod of tyranny, become equally hardened by the exercise of cruelty, and equally insensible to the sufferings of their fellow men. Such is the nature and tendency of despotism, that in its operation, it not only checks the progress of civilization, but actually converts the civilized man into a savage; at least so far as respects the humane affections of the heart.

In ancient Rome, parents had the most despotic power over their children. By the laws of Romulus, confirmed by the laws of the twelve tables, fathers might or even slay their children.† The same absolute authority had masters over their slaves;‡ tho before the close of the Republic this power was abridged by the Cornelian Law, and was finally abolished by the Emperor Adrian.

These unlimited powers exercised by the old Romans, together with their martial life, and the constant view of the combats of the gladiators, which habituated them to scenes of blood and cruelty,

---

* The negroes in the West Indies consider death as a deliverance from servitude and a restoration to their native country. Hence their funerals are scenes of joy and festivity, and are attended with dancing.

† In liberos suprema patrum auctoritas esto; venumdare, occidere licet. Leg. Rom. This power of the father over his children was restrained by imperial constitutions before the times of Justinian. See Justin Inst. lib. 1. tit. 9.

‡ Justin. Inst. lib. 1. tit. 8.

inspired them with a barbarous fierceness, which prepared them for the practice of public plunder and private affassination.† But were the Romans more cruel by nature than modern nations? Were they more savage in their tempers than the lordly despots of the present age, who are accustomed to tyranize over slaves? " Do we not perceive," says that judicious traveller Dr. Moore,‡ " that the practice of domestic slavery has, at this day, a strong tendency to render men haughty, capricious and cruel? Such is the nature of man, that if he has power without controul, he will use it without justice ; absolute power has a strong tendency to make good men bad, and never fails to make bad men worse."

It may be remarked that with respect to a great number of vices, the extremes of society approach very near each other. The tyrant is above law, and his slave is below it. Men, in excess of happiness or misery," says Montesquieu.§ are equally inclinable to severity ; witness conquerors and monks." He might have extended the remark to *masters* and *slaves*, who in general are equally lazy, cruel and ferocious. So with respect to excessive gaming, says Millar, in his historical view of the English Government,‖ which is a vice peculiarly predominant in the most rude and barbarous, as well as the most luxurious and opulent nations.* The same observation may be made with respect to excessive drinking. The progress of power and wealth in civilized states may, as it respects the prevalence of these and some other vices, be resembled to a circle ; making the equal poverty and independence of the savage state the point at which the progress begins and pursuing it to the opposite point, we have that state of society in which mediocrity of fortune and power give lenity to government and mildness to manners ; but in pursuing the progress further, we find great wealth and power with excessive poverty, and society, with a retrogradual motion, approaching the original point of barbarism. An extreme disparity of circumstances renders one class of men the masters of the other, and the *tyrant*, and his *slave* in their cruelty, their stubborness, their laziness, their inhumanity, and their excessive passion for revenge become allied to savages. Whatever exceptions there may be to this rule, it is generally true that the possession of power renders men proud, insolent, cruel vindictive ; and the reason why this character is not applicable, in its full extent, to American planters who are owners of slaves, is not that Americans are born with better hearts than other men, or that the nature of domestic tyranny is changed, but it is because the imme-

† Montesq. Reflections on the causes of the rise and fall of the Roman Empire. p. 118.
‡ vol. 1. p. 212. where the reader will find some excellent remarks on this subject. See also Hume's Essays vol. 1. p. 402.
§ Spirit of Laws, book 6. chap. 9. ‖ page 30. 31.
* Tacitus de Mor. Germ. ca. 24. 22.
†† The editor of Watson's Philip. ad remarks that " ideas of superior dignity have a tendency to blunt the sense of injustice committed against inferiors." page 408. note.

diate exercise of despotism is delegated to substitutes. The negro driver is generally the active tyrant, and acquires all the ferocious qualities connected with his profession.

It is remarkable likewise that a spirit of private revenge is more prevalent among the little tyrants who are educated with slaves, than among the citizens of a free state where there is little distinction of rank and power. I refer in particular to the custom of duelling, which is merely a savage spirit of revenge, set in motion by a squeamish delicacy about trifles and regulated by certain rules of refinement falsely called *laws of honor*. This custom, which had its origin in the dark ages of European savageness, when the right of private revenge and hostility was in full exercise,* is retained in all parts of Europe and America, where slavery exists, and is nearly or totally banished from states where there is full liberty and equality of rights among all the citizens. Every year brings us news of the fatal effects of this savage practice in the southern States of America ; but in the eastern states the practice can be hardly said to exist. To the honor of the laws, the institutions, and the manners of this state, be it remembered, that no instance of this barbarous custom has yet stained the annals of our Republic."

The exercise of uncontrolled power, always gives a peculiar complexion to the manners, passions and conversation both of the oppressor and the oppressed.

The tyrant is rough, boisterous, irritable—he takes fire at a word or a wink, and blood must satiate his vengeance. In moderate governments, men are taught to moderate their passions and pretensions ; by the diffusion of power, its force is divided and weakened ; every man's right is controuled by the equal right of his neighbor, as well as by the laws ; equality of rights begets mutual respect, and respect begets affability, condescension and mildness of manners.†

The character of the inhabitants in almost all free republican states, where domestic slavery does not exist, verifies these remarks. The natives of the free Swiss Cantons, possess frankness and hospi-

---

* Millar's hist. view of the Engl. gov. p. 62. The practice of private stabbing, formerly so common in England, and still frequent in Spain, and some other countries, may be traced to this source ; but universal liberty and science will banish it from the earth.

† Men are better and more amiable, in proportion as they are happier. Moderate independence banishes care and disposes the mind to joy and beneficence. Bourg. travels vol. 1. 383. The character of the Swiss in the free Cantons, and of the New-England people, is a full proof of this doctrine ; but the most illustrious example of the effects of equal rights among men, is the peaceable disposition of the Quakers. It is curious to mark the different effects which steady laws and the arbitrary exercise of will have upon the manners of men. The government of the Quakers is very absolute and rigid ; but it is the authority of *laws* and *rules*, and not of *arbitrary will*; therefore *steady* in its operation. Hence the firm, uniform, systematic deportment of the members of that society. A Quaker is seldom capricious, or irritable ; but moderate in his passions, slow in deciding, and very persevering. How different is a man born in the same nation, who has been accustomed to brandish his whip over slaves.

tality, with great civility of manners. They bow to paſſengers,
not with an air of mean ſervility, but like well bred men, conſcious
of their independence.* In Sweden, where the peaſantry enjoy
ſome property and many privileges, travellers have remarked nearly the ſame traits of character in the lower orders of people.

Aſtoniſhingly different is the character of the Poliſh peaſants.
The latter, who are ſubject to the moſt unlimited tyranny, are
cringing and ſervile in their language and manners ; when ſtrangers
paſs by them, they bow down to the ground ; at the firſt glimpſe of a
gentleman's carriage, they ſtop their carts and taking off their hats or
caps, hold them in their hands, till the gentleman is out of ſight.†
Such manners mark in a ſtriking degree, the abject ſervitude, by
which theſe pitiable peaſants are humbled and depreſſed.

The tendency of tyranny, both civil and domeſtic, to annihilate
the ſocial affections, or abridge their operation, is very remarkable
in its effect upon *hoſpitality*. In a ſavage ſtate, hoſpitality is extended to all men, without diſtinction. Among the antient Germans,
it was deemed a crime to refuſe entertainment to any of the human
race. Every man who travelled among them, whether ſtranger or
friend, was received with equal and liberal hoſpitality, and at his
departure, he was gratified with whatever he requeſted.‖ Such is
the univerſal practice among the aborigines of America ; there is
no inſtance in which hoſpitality has been refuſed to Europeans, un-
leſs the Indian natives have been firſt abuſed or provoked to hoſtili-
ty by the treachery of civilized ſtrangers.

Hoſpitality is the moſt inartificial of all the virtues. It may be
conſidered as *natural*, for its exerciſe flows immediately from in-
ſtinct. That men are all *brethren*, the children of one common father, is an impreſſion of nature ; and the heart of man in a ſtate of
primæval ſimplicity, untainted with prejudice, uncorrupted by
intereſt, every where recognizes the alliance of nature, and clings
to its kindred man.

Not ſo the artificial being, whom fortune or accident has elevated above his brethren. The nabob and the tyrant, educated in
the practice of commanding, perhaps of abuſing their unfortunate
ſlaves, very early loſe the ſympathies of their nature, and acquire a
habit of deſpiſing all who are placed in meaner circumſtances. Contempt deſtroys hoſpitality, and thus it happens that the rich and
powerful uſually confine their hoſpitable attentions to thoſe of their
own rank. The more elevated the man on the pyramid of power,
the farther is he removed from the reſt of the human race ; the
ſmaller is the circle of his equals, and the leſs extenſive is the ſphere
of his perſonal attachments. Thus the inequalities of ſociety,
which are always the greateſt where ſlavery is permitted, tend di-
rectly to circumſcribe the exerciſe of that diffuſive benevolence,
which nature dictates and chriſtanity enjoins The untutored ſavage
takes a ſtranger by the hand, and ſeats him at his hoſpitable board,
with a hearty welcome, merely becauſe he is a *man*; the haughty

* Coxe's Switz. vol. 1. 27. 46. Vol. 2. 201.
† Coxe's travels, vol. 1. 279. ‖Tacitus.

nabob admits, for guests, the choice few who have rank and titles, and with a contemptuous pride, shuts his doors against the rest of mankind.*

But in no particular are the deplorable effects of slavery more visible, than in checking, or destroying national industry. Where-ever we turn our eyes to view the comparative effects of freedom and slavery on agriculture, arts, commerce and science, the mind is deeply affected at the astonishing contrast.

About the 11th century, the feudal system was established with nearly an equal degree of rigor, in all the kingdoms of Europe. As to the state of the peasantry and of agriculture at that period, England and Poland were nearly in the same situation. The *serfs* of Poland and the *churles* of England were slaves, incapable of acquiring property and annexed to manors like the stock of a farm, much in the same manner as the negroes are at this day in the West Indies and Southern American States. From that period to this time, the peasantry of Poland have continued in the same state with little amelioration of their condition. But the churles in England have been more fortunate. To trace the particular steps by which the churles and villains of England were raised from their abject servitude, to the present state of the farmers in that country, does not fall within my design ;† it is sufficient to remark that gradual means, they have become free tenants, who have a legal prop-erty in the estates which they cultivate. Instead of being tenants at will and liable to be turned out of their possessions at any moment by their capricious lords, they have a permanent interest in their estates, which the laws of the country protect, and transmit to their heirs. This is the principal circumstance which has rendered the agriculture of England flourishing, and the farmers more in-telligent, wealthy and respectable than the miserable serfs in Po-land.

To labor solely for the benefit of other men, is repugnant to ev-ery principle of the human heart. Men will not be industrious, nor is it the will of heaven that they should be, without a well founded expectation of enjoying the fruits of their labor. The ag-riculture of a country therefore will always be flourishing and pro-ductive, in proportion to the quantity and duration of interest which the farmers have in the lands they cultivate,‡ combined with the security of enjoying the produce, without arbitrary taxation or grievous assessments. That country produces most where the farmers are freeholders, possessing the fee simple of their lands, pay-ing little or no rent, and light taxes. That country produces least,

* Luxuries and an abuse of civilization contract and debase the mind. Bourg. Travels. vol. 1. p. 383. And See vol. 2. p. 137. Essays on Spain by Mon. Peyron.
† See Millar's hist view of the Eng. Gov. p. 183. Blacks. Com. vol. 2. p. 90. and the histories of England.
‡ The natural soil, markets &c. being equal. See some excellent remarks on this subject in Smith's Wealth of Nations. Book 3. ch. 2. Robertson's Ind. page 288. Bourg. Travels in Spain. vol. 2. 90.

where the cultivators are slaves, who have no interest in their own labors, and who work only by compulsion. Between these extremes, the productiveness of a country is in proportion to the length of the leases of the farms, the smallness of the rent and the lightness of the taxes and imposts. A tenant who has a lease for several hundred years, at a small fixed rent, not liable to be encreased at the pleasure of the landlord, has an interest in his farm almost equivalent to a fee simple. A tenant for life, who has little expectation that his heirs will enjoy his farm, is under strong temptations to make the most of the land for himself, at the expense of the soil, the buildings and fences. Instead of making improvement, he will probably impoverish the land and leave the buildings and fences out of repair. The tenant at will has still less interest in the land he occupies, and if, as in Turkey, he is subject to the arbitrary exactions of Pachas, Governors, landlords or collectors of revenue, who take his earnings from him at pleasure, he has no more encouragement to labor than the slave, and of course he will look no farther than to make provision for the moment.

The past and present state of the world, verifies these remarks. By the antient laws or customs of Ireland, before the introduction of the English laws after the conquest of Henry II, the lands were held by the singular tenures of *tanistry* and *gavelkind*. By the custom of tanistry, when a nobleman died, his castles, manors and lands descended to the *oldest and most worthy of his blood and surname*. It was often uncertain who, of the blood and surname of the last possessor, was the *most worthy*; and from this uncertainty arose competitions for the inheritance, which not unfrequently ended in civil war.

By the custom of gavelkind, the canfinny or chief of a lineage, which was called a sept, made all the partitions of land, belonging to the tanist, at his discretion. When a ter-tenant died, the chief assembled all the sept, and throwing all the farms into common stock, made a new distribution; allotting to each the best or greatest portion, according to his seniority. These assignments were made by the chief *ex arbitrio*, on the death of every ter-tenant, and of consequence, the translations of each tenant from one possession to another were so frequent, that the cultivators of the earth had no security for the enjoyment of their lands, even for a month.† The effect was what we should expect; no comfortable habitations were erected; no enclosure or improvement was made of the lands where these customs prevailed, especially in the province of Ulster, which was little better than one vast wilderness. This was a principal cause of the poverty and barbarism which formerly prevailed in Ire-

† A similar custom prevailed among the antient Germans. Their reasons as assigned by the historian, were to prevent the people from attaching themselves to agriculture, in preference to war, and from amassing great estates at the expense of the poor, from enervating themselves by living in good houses, &c. See Cæsars comment. lib. 6, ¶. 20.

land.[*] These customs were abolished in the reign of James the first, and the lands in Ireland, were, by solemn adjudications of the court of Kings bench in that country, declared to be descendible according to the common law of England. But still the lords of manors oppress and grind the cultivators of the soil, and in no part of Europe, are the peasantry more poor and wretched, and in few countries, is the earth under worse cultivation than in Ireland.

If we turn our eyes to the continent of Europe, we shall see the progress of agriculture, of arts and every species of improvement, very nearly proportioned to the freedom of the people. In the Bavarian and some other circles of Germany, we behold a peasantry lazy and vicious, agriculture languishing, some of the largest cities declining, and the roads and inns wearing marks of the political oppressions suffered by the inhabitants.[‡] In the hereditary dominions of the house of Austria, we see evident marks of the attention of government to the welfare of the people. Agriculture, commerce and the arts in *Austria proper*, are in a better condition than in many parts of Germany ; at the same time, we abhor the partiality of the princes of that illustrious house, who form regulations for the purpose of drawing wealth from their conquered provinces to enrich their family possessions. Pursuing our views farther eastward, into the conquered countries, we behold in Hungary and Bohemia, a soil naturally fertile, lying waste, and uncultivated, under the civil oppression of the nobility and the political restrictions of the house of Austria. Here vast tracts of country are desolate, and the eye is offended with the unnatural contrast of splendid riches, surrounded with extreme poverty ; here and there palaces of marble, towering to the sky, and all the rest of the country a dreary waste, or covered with filthy hovels of a forlorn peasantry. To the northward, the electorate of Saxony, whose soil, tho barren, is possessed by men enjoying a portion of freedom, relieves the eye with an appearance of an active, industrious contented peasantry, a growing commerce and neat well built, flourishing cities ; the vallies thickly dotted with populous villages, and the mountains covered with sheep.

Extending our view to Prussia, we see a country just arisen from obscurity to a splendid rank among the powers of the earth, by the efforts of a single man. We behold that singular phenomenon, an absolute monarch, exercising a most unlimited sway over his dominions, with the view of rendering his subjects wealthy and happy, and his country flourishing and respectable.[†] The great Frederick, not only defended and enlarged his dominions, but he

* See Sir John Davies reports, p. 78. 134. Hume's Essays, vol. 1. p. 461. In Andalusia in Spain, a few proprietors possess almost the whole country. Unable to cultivate such immense estates, they farm out land on *short* leases, and the whole province is little better than a desert. See Bourg. travels in Spain, vol. 2. p. 91. 92.
‡ Riesbecks Travels vol. 1.
† The happiness of a people under a despotic government depends mostly on the *character* of the prince. Moore's Italy. p. 137.

formed and established a system of internal police and political econo-
omy, much more beneficial to his subjects than his victories and
acquisitions of territory. From his own extensive demain, he se-
parated innumerable farms which he granted to his subjects in hereditary succession, at a small annual rent; thus converting a
number of idle soldiers and poor men into industrious freeholders.
He procured the seed of the most valuable grasses, and distributed
gratuitously among his subjects; and by these and other encourage-
ments, the barren sands of his dominions were soon changed into
fruitful fields. To remove the causes of disease, he drained marshes,
opened forests and restrained the inundations of rivers. He annually bestowed large sums for the encouragement of manufactures,
as well as agriculture; he joined rivers by navigable canals; favored the importation of necessaries and restrained that of luxuries;
he established schools for the education of the peasants; courted
and rewarded men of literary merit; and such was his success,
that during his reign, the population, and the wealth of his dominions were doubled.[*] What a glorious example is this! and what a
reproach to the great and little tyrants who surround the Prus-
sian territories, and who know no use of their power, but to squeeze
and plunder their subjects.

Ranging still farther eastward, the eye rests upon the kingdom of
Poland, where a complicated political and civil despotism clouds
and darkens the prospect. Until the reign of Cassimir the great, in
the 14th century, a lord could put his peasant to death with impu-
nity; and when the latter died without children, the lord considered himself as his heir, and siezed all his effects. Cassimir, in 1347,
prescribed a fine for the murder of a peasant, and enacted that if
one died without issue, his next heir should inherit. But these sa-
lutary laws, calculated to alleviate the miseries of the peasantry,
were eluded by the powerful and licentious nobles. It was not till
1768 that the statutes of Poland made it a capital crime to murder a
peasant; and even now, it requires such an accumulation of evidence
to convict the offender, that the law is rendered almost nugatory.[†]

What then must be the situation of agriculture, arts and commerce in Poland? What must necessarily be the appearance of the
country, where men are thus treated like cattle? Let us hear the
affecting description of it given by that sensible and judicious traveller Mr. Coxe. "I never, says he,[‡] saw a road so barren of in-
teresting scenes, as that from Cracow to Warsaw. The country
was chiefly overspread with vast tracts of thick gloomy forest.
Without having actually traversed it, I could hardly have conceiv-
ed so comfortless a region. A forlorn stillness and solitude prevailed
almost thro the whole extent, with few symptoms of an inhabited,

---

* See Gillies view of the reign of Frederick II, ch. 7. Riesbeck's travels
vol. 2. p. 88 to 202.
† Coxe's travels vol. 1, 156. 158.
‡ Travels into Poland, &c. vol. 1. p. 290.

and still lefs of a civilized country. Tho we travelled in the high road, which unites Cracow and Warfaw, in the courfe of about 258 Englifh miles, we met in our progrefs, only two carriages, and abc it a dozen carts. The country was equally thin of human habitations ; a few ftraggling villages, all built of wood, fucceeded one another at long intervals, whofe miferable appearance correfponded to the wretchednefs of the country around them. In thefe affemblages of huts, the only places of reception for travellers were hovels, belonging to Jews, totally deftitute of furniture and every fpecies of accommodation. We could feldom procure any other room than that in which the family lived ; in the article of provifion, eggs and milk were our greateft luxuries and could not always be obtained ; our only bed was ftraw thrown upon the ground, and we thought ourfelves happy when we could procure it clean. The natives were poorer, humbler and more miferable than any people we had yet obferved in our travels. Whenever we ftopped, they flocked around us in crouds, and with the moft abject geftures, begged for charity."

Cafting our eyes, from this difgufting fpectable, towards the immenfe empire of Ruffia in the north, nearly the fame difmal appearances are prefented to our view. The defpotifm of a half-barbarous nobility concurs with the arbitrary nature of the government, to pillage and debafe the ferfs, and render them humble, obftinate, theivifh, improvident and infenfible. Here induftry is checked and difcouraged by the arbitrary exactions of the great proprietors of land, whofe power over their vaffals is without controul. A direct tax is laid upon the virtues of induftry and frugality by a rapacious nobility, who affefs their peafants in proportion to their fuppofed profits, tho the poor wretches are incapable of acquiring and holding property. Thus a mafon or fmith, who is a good workman, is often rated as high as 6, 12 and even 20l. fterling a year. It is however fome alleviation to a benevolent mind, to fee the fovereigns of that almoft boundlefs empire, exerting their power for the benefit of their fubjects. The prefent emprefs, perceiving the true caufe of the languifhing ftate of commerce, arts and agriculture in her dominions,† has attempted to remedy the evil by multiplying the numbers and enlarging the privileges of the merchants, burghers and other freemen, who formerly were in a condition very little better than the flaves—by waving feveral rights of the crown, and facilitating the means of obtaining freedom—and by eftablifhing in 1765 the *Free Economical Society*, or fociety for the promotion of agriculture with extenfive privileges.

From the frigid regions of Ruffia, let us caft our eyes fouthward over the vaft territories where the Turkifh Sultan, with the Koran and the Saber, impofes law upon his numerous millions. Here the political profpect thickens into deep melancholy memphi-

† " L' agriculture ne pourra jamais profperer la ou l' agriculteur ne poffede rien en propre." Inftructions for a new code of laws, p. 83. See Coxe's travels- book 5. ch. 5 and 6,

an gloom. Egypt and Phenicia, Greece and Syria, the parents and the nurses of science, arts and commerce, are now doomed to be the prey of superstition and tyranny. Here the mufti, with his infallible Koran ; the Cadi with his arbitrary decisions; the Publican with his extortion, and the Pacha with his janazaries, exercise a heterogeneous despotism, which is neither limited by laws, nor controlled by precedents.

Here slavery assumes a different form. The conquered natives of the Ottoman dominions are not subject to a feudal servitude ; they are not the *adscriptitii glebæ* of ancient Rome, or modern Poland and Russia. But they are subject to the worst species of bondage, the arbitrary and capricious exactions of numberless petty tyrants, the collectors of taxes and governors of provinces, whose rapaciousness is restrained by no superior power, and the precarious tenure of whose offices tempts them to harrass the people with immoderate demands, that they may fill their own purses while the power is in their hands.

When Sultan Selim first made a conquest of Syria, in order to favor the husbandman, whose worth he knew, he established the *miri*, a territorial tribute, which was fixed at a certain rate that was not to be augmented or diminished. This tribute was moderate, and had it not been for the abuses of the Turkish government, it never could have oppressed the people. But the Pachas who have most of the lands at their disposal, take care, when they make grants, to clog them with burthensome conditions ; they exact the half or even two thirds of the crop : they monopolize the seed and the cattle, so that the cultivators are compelled to purchase from them at their own price. When the harvest is over, they cavil about losses and pretended robberies, and as they have the power in their hands, they carry off what they think proper. If the season fails, they exact the same sum, and to raise this they expose to sale every thing the poor peasant possesses. Happily his person remains free, for the Turks are ignorant of the refinement of imprisoning for debt, when the man has no longer any property.

These oppressions are constant, and to these is added a multitude of occasional extortions. Sometimes a whole village is laid under contribution for some offence, real or imaginary. A present is demanded on the accession of each new governor ; a contribution of grass is required for his horses, and of straw and barley for his cavaliers, and all the soldiers who pass must be provided for by the poor peasants. The Villages tremble when a soldier appears, as they would at the approach of a robber. He enters as a conqueror and commands as a master ; " *dogs, rabble,*" he cries, " *bread, coffee, tobacco; I must have barley, I must have meat.*" If he casts his eyes on poultry, he kills them, and at his departure, he adds insult to tyranny. In vain do the peasants exclaim against this injustice ; the saber imposes silence ; justice is remote and difficult of access ; nay complaints are even dangerous.

What is the consequence of these depredations ? The poorer

clafs of inhabitants, ruined and unable to pay the tribute, forfoke
the villages and fly to the cities. But the tribute of the village
cannot be diminished; the fum to be levied muft be found; the
burthen therefore falls with accumulated weight on the remaining
inhabitants, and becomes infupportable. A two years drouth ruins
the village, the inhabitants abandon it, and the tax it fhould have
paid is levied on the neighboring lands.

It is remarked that thefe exactions have made a rapid progrefs,
during the laft 40 years, from which period the people date the
decline of agriculture, the depopulation of the country, and the
diminution of the Sultans revenue.*

The fituation of the peafants is wretched beyond defcription.
They are every where reduced to a little cake of barley, onions, len-
tils and water. In the mountains of Lebanon, they ufe acorns for
food, after boiling or roafting them on the afhes.

In confequence of the mifery of the hufbandman, and the precarious ftate of his property, cultivation is neglected. The farmer's
plow is frequently no more than the branch of a tree, cut below a
bifurcation. The country is tilled by affes and cows; rarely by
oxen. On the borders of Arabia, the countryman, for fear of the
wild Arabs, muft fow with his mufket in his hand; and when his
corn turns yellow, and before it is ripe he muft reap it and hide it
in fubterranean caverns. In a word, the induftry of the country is
limited to a fupply of immediate wants; to procure a little bread
and a few onions, a wretched blue fhirt and a bit of woollen cloth.
The peafant indeed lives in fear and diftrefs, but it is a confolation
that he does not enrich his tyrants, and that the avarice of defpotifm inflicts its own punifhment.

The arts, fciences and commerce throughout the Turkifh empire
have fhared the fame fate as agriculture. The manufactures of the
people are confined to a few articles of cloathing and arms, their
reading extends only to the Koran, a few monkifh books and legen-
dary tales, and their little commerce is in the hands of Franks,
Greeks and Arminians. Moft of the harbors on the coaft of Egypt,
Syria, Afia Minor, and the Greek Iflands, are choaked up with
fand; the Levant is infefted with pirates; and the depopulation of
fome of the moft fertile provinces of the Ottoman empire, exhibits
the fatal effects of the wide-wafting peftilential power of a ferocious government.

Yet even in the dark and defolate regions of tyranny, a few
fcattering rays of liberty arife and cheer the melancholy profpect.
On the barren mountains of Syria, between Lebanon and the val-
ley of Bekaa, are the Maronites and Druzes, who have been able
to preferve themfelves from the iron rod of Ottoman power, on the
eafy condition of paying a fmall annual tribute to the neighboring
Pachas. Here defended by their inacceffible rocks and their va-
lour, they live unmolefted by tyrants; the inhabitants are moftly
freeholders, who enjoy the fruits of their labor and they have con-

---

* See Volney's Travels. Vol. 2. Ch. 37.

verted their barren hills into productive vineyards.† To thefe
may be added the inhabitants of a little Ifland called Caios on the
coaft of Natolia, not more than three leagues in circumference,
whofe poverty and inacceffibility with the privateers of Malta have
fecured to them their freedom and independence. In thefe little
fpots of earth, which have efcaped the devouring and debafing influence of defpotifm, the traveller finds among the inhabitants moſt
of the noble qualities of primitive man. Brave, honeft, active, humane, affable, faithful, hofpitable and induftrious : Such are the
inhabitants of the fmall diftricts which have retained their freedom
and property, amidft the cruelties, the wars, the tumults and the
devaftations of the Mahometan empire.‡

From a view of the deplorable ftate of men under the Turkifh
government, let us caft our eyes on Italy, once the feat of the
greateft empire on earth. Here indeed the peafantry are lefs
wretched ; but as all the lands belong to the nobility, the clergy
and the convents, and the laboring poor receive little benefit from
their induftry, agriculture languifhes, and the fineft country on
earth is covered with idlers and vagabonds. Here fuperftition
erects her throne, and numberlefs fantaftic ceremonies ferve to amufe
a biggotted populace. The loitering fons of want, ragged and poor,
fpend their time in counting their beads, bowing to proceffions,
chanting *te deum*, or gaping at the liquefaction of St. Januarius's
blood and other tricks of prieftcraft ; then ftrolling away to fome
convent, they beg a little portion of food, and become half infenfible to the mifery of their condition.§ Sicily, that luxuriant fpot
of earth which once poured forth corn enough to feed Rome when
miftrefs of the world, now lies half cultivated under the oppreffive
reftrictions of a tyrannical polic ... defpotifm, blind and head-
ftrong, often commits fuicide. ... ly, where, with ordinary
cultivation, a fingle harveft will fur...h wheat enough for a feven
years fubfiftence of its inhabitants, the exportation of that article is
prohibited to all who cannot pay an exorbitant price for the privilege. The confequence is inevitable—the hufbandman gathers
with a heavy heart, his abundant harveft, with a profpect of lofing a
great part of his labor ; and Sicily is impoverifhed in the midft of
plenty.‖

From this delightful region, where nature has beftowed her richeft charms only to be rifled by the rough hand of defpotifm, let us
advance and climb the Alps, where deep vales and woods, ftagnant
lakes, barren rocks, and towering cliffs exalting their fnow encircled
tops above the clouds, checker the face of nature's works. Here
the political profpect changes, and to the ftatefman, prefents a fcene

† Volneys travels. vol. 2. chap. 24. ‡ Savary's Letters on Grece. p. 119.
§ Moore's view of fociety and manners in Italy. Letter. 73 and 59.
There are 30,000 lazzaroni in Naples, who have no houfes or property.
They fleep under porticos, piazzas, or any other fhelter.
‖ Brydon's Tour. vol. 2. p. 42. 187. The Duke of Lerma, minifter of
Philip 3 King of Spain, drew from Sicily, in wheat only, an annual value of
72,000 ducats. Watfon's Philip 3. 143.

as enchanting, as it is fublime anft magnificent. This is the region of freedom. Here the honeft hardy Swifs plants and prunes his vines—feeds his flock or whiftles along the furrow, peaceable and fecure. Here no lordly mafter, no grinding fteward or overfeer, no Turkifh foldier or Pacha, with his drawn faber, demands the hard earned fruits of the peafants labor. The farmer, lord of his own foil, plants his corn with cheerfulnefs and contentment, becaufe the produce will be his own. Here cold moraffes and barren hills are converted into productive fields by the plaftic power of induftry. The mountains covered with herds of cattle or clothed with luxuriant vines, the valleys checkered with fields of grain, and fprinkled with well built villages, all announce the eafe, fecurity and independence of the inhabitants, and proclaim to the world that the Swifs are *free*.

Cafting our eyes on Spain, we fee a country governed by monks, fryars and tyrants; genius cramped; and the freedom of opinions reftrained by an inquifitorial jealoufy; commerce monopolized or fhackled by the fovereign; a fertile kingdom depopulated by civil and religious oppreffion, and beggared by the very poffeffion of half the gold and filver of the world.‡

Proceeding to France, we behold the moft interefting fpectacle ever exhibited on the theater of this earth; a great and enlightened people ftruggling, not only to break down the feudal and hierarchal fyftems of defpotifm, but to exterminate their very principles, remove the gothic rubbifh from their extenfive territory, and prepare the foil for the more generous plant of liberty. Before the late revolution, the rigor of the feudal tenures in France, was confiderably relaxed; the peafantry had rifen to the rank of Metayers, or Coloni Partiarii; the proprietors of the land furnifhing the feed, the utenfils and the whole ftock of the farm, and the produce being equally divided between the proprietor and the cultivator. Farmers of this kind have a much greater intereft in their own labor than flaves, they are freemen and can acquire property. But their intereft is not fufficient to encourage agricultural improvement. The payment of *tithe* or a *tenth* of the produce is found in Europe to be a great hindrance to the progrefs of agriculture; a tax of one *half* the produce muft therefore be an effectual bar to it. It is the intereft of the farmer to make the land produce as much as poffible, by means of the ftock furnifhed by the proprietor; but never to encreafe that ftock by the favings out of his own fhare of the produce. It is ftill more his intereft to ufe the landlords cattle in other bufinefs. It was obferved in France before the revolution, that the matayers took every opportunity of employing the proprietors cattle in carriage, rather than in cultivation; becaufe the profits of *tranfportation* were all their own, whereas the produce of the land was divided equally between themfelves and the proprietor.§

---

† See Coxe's Switzerland. paffim. ‡ Bourgoanne's prefent State of Spain. vol. 1. p. 253. 155. 276.
§ Smith's wealth of nations book 3. ch. 2.

France however, by means of her peculiar fertility of soil, falubrity of climate, and many excellent institutions and focieties, together with the meliorated condition of her peasantry, was, before the revolution, advanced far beyond Spain, and many parts of Germany, in agricultural improvement, as well as in fcience. What effect the revolution will have upon the progrefs of improvement, we may predict with a good degree of certainty. By the fequeftration of the royal demains, and the immenfe poffeffions belonging to the regular and fecular clergy, together with the forfeited eftates of the temporal nobility, who have deferted their country, an almoft total change of property has taken place; and throughout that vaft Republic, millions of independent freeholders will arife, who, poffeffing the whole eftate or intereft in the lands they cultivate, will have every poffible motive for introducing the higheft ftate of improvement. It is reported that already the revolution has given a new fpring to national induftry.* But more time and more ftable government are neceffary to produce any effential alteration in the face of that country. At all events, fome great changes, agricultural and commercial as well as political, will follow the revolution; and France has now an opportunity of making a diftinguifhed and glorious experiment in favor of national induftry and public happinefs. Let us then drop a tear over the calamities that attend the French revolution, calamities infeparable from fuch great changes and events; let candor find fome apology for the riots and outrages of a licentious populace, in the treachery and perjuries of their perfidious domeftic foes; let reafon fmile at the profpect of peace in that new born republic, when a freely-elected houfe of reprefentatives fhall collect the juft wifhes of 25,000,000 of freemen; when an elective fenate, diftinguifhed from the commons only by the venerable age and experience of its members, fhall check the ardor and precipitance of a popular affembly and give ftability to their legiflative proceedings; and when an energetic executive fhall be conftituted by the unbiaffed fuffrages of enlightened citizens, armed with the whole power of the nation to enforce the refolutions of the legiflature.

From a profpect fo flattering, let us turn our eyes upon Great Britain, where a brave people have purchafed, with their blood, and defended with firmnefs, a larger portion of freedom and a more excellent conftitution of government than have been enjoyed by any of the great nations of Europe. Here we fee the glorious effects of liberty, of fixed laws and fecure property. Here is a fubftantial body of freeholders, the ftrength and foul of a nation; here numerous manufactories employ fuperfluous hands, feed the poor and convert every fpecies of raw materials into gold; here arts and fcience, patronized and nourifhed, exalt the human mind and add national fame to national wealth; while fleets and navies protect her fea-furrounded dominions, and waft her productions round the globe.

* Before the revolution, agriculture in France was lefs productive than in England, in the proportion of 3 to 8.

Yet the pleasure we receive from this prospect is not without alloy. Some great estates, which have continued unbroken from the times of feudal anarchy,* are not yet cultivated to the degree of which they are susceptible; many cities and boroughs hold chartered rights and exclusive privileges repugnant to the spirit of the constitution and destructive of national prosperity; while the laws of the kingdom, with an intolerant spirit, which is the scourge of freedom, proscribe, from the rights of society, certain denominations of subjects, for maintaining opinions which no human tribunal can control, and which are as harmless in government as the dreams of the night.

Wishing long peace and prosperity to our parent state, and a quiet repeal of her antichristian intolerant laws, let us return to our native country, and with tranquil delight, contemplate that happy portion of freedom and that rational government allotted to the United States of America. Here the mind of man, as free as the air he breathes, may exert all its energy, and by expanding its powers to distant and various objects, its faculties may be enlarged to a degree hitherto unknown. Here the equalizing genius of the laws distributes property to every citizen; here all religious opinions are equally harmless and render men equally good subjects, because there are no laws to oppose and control them; here no tithes, no rack rents, no lordly exactions of gratuities and fines for alienation, no arbitrary impositions of taxes, harrass the cultivator of the soil and repress his exertions. Here no beggarly monks and fryars, no princely ecclesiastics with their annual income of millions, no idle court-pensioners and titled mendicants, no spies to watch and betray the unsuspecting citizen, no tyrant with his train of hounds, bastards and mistresses, those vultures of government, prey upon the poor peasant and exhaust the public treasury of the nation. Here no commercial or corporation monopolies give exclusive advantages to favored individuals, and extinguish the ardor of national enterprize; no sacramental test bars the conscientious sectary from places of trust and emolument, or tempts him to dissimulation and perjury; here no monasteries, convents and nunneries, the retreats of idleness and the nurseries of superstition and debauchery; no monkish principles of celibacy; no daily ceremonies of processions, and mock-miracles divert the minds of men from the occupations of industry, or check the population of the country. Here every man finds employment, and the road is open for the poorest citizen to amass wealth by labor and economy, and by his talents and virtue to raise himself to the highest offices of State. Here the laws provide for the poor, whom age or infirmity has deprived of the power of obtaining subsistence, and beggary is banished from our doors.‡ Here

---

* Smith's Wealth of Nations. Book 3. Ch. 2.

‡ This is almost literally true in this State; and as it respects the natives of the United States, it is true in most of the other States. The laws of Connecticut oblige every town to support its own poor. If any man is ever distressed with want, he can call upon the town for aid, and demand support. But the poor are not numerous.

the children of the poorest citizen have accefs to fchools at the public expense ; the eftablifhment of numerous parifh or other private libraries, with the univerfal circulation of newfpapers, pamphlets and magazines has diffufed a competent knowledge of religion, arts and government among the fubftantial inhabitants ; while academies and univerfities, well endowed and furnifhed with able profeffors, nourifh the fciences and prepare our youth for the pulpit, the bar and the caßinet.* Here population has exceeded all European calculations ; already has the active genius of America begun manufacturing eftablifhments ; already do her fhips traverfe the globe, and collect wealth on the ocean and the iflands, from the Straits of Magellan to the inhofpitable regions of Kamchatska ; and in the fhort period of 170 years, fince our anceftors landed on thefe fhores, a tracklefs wildernefs, inhabited only by favages and wild beafts, is converted into fruitful fields and meadows, more highly cultivated than one half of Europe.

But while we indulge the pleafure of viewing this animating profpect, let us not forget that of 4,000,000 of Inhabitants in the United States, almoft 700,000 are flaves ; a circumftance which cannot fail to allay the joy, that the profperous ftate of the country would otherwife infpire in every patriotic bofom. Deteftable was the policy which firft introduced the practice of cultivating plantations by flaves ; and both in a political and moral veiw, deplorable are the confequences of that policy !

But fince the evil really exifts, it becomes a queftion of infinite magnitude, what effectual remedy can be applied, confiftent with that regard to private property and public fafety and honor, which ought ever to direct our national councils.

That freedom is the facred right of every man whatever be his color, who has not forfeited it by fome violation of municipal law, is a truth eftablifhed by God himfelf in the very creation of human beings. No time, no circumftances, no human power or policy can change the nature of this truth, nor repeal the fundamental laws of fociety by which every man's right to liberty is guaranteed. The firft act therefore of enflaving men is always a violation of thofe great primary laws of fociety, by which alone the mafter himfelf holds every particle of his own freedom.

But are there not cafes when it is neceffary to make a diftinction between *abftract right and political expedience ?* Is it not true that *political expedience,* properly underftood, is the foundation of all *public right and juftice ?* The African flave trade originated when political and focial rights were not generally underftood, and when the few philofophers who underftood and attempted to defend them could make a very feeble refiftance to the fuggeftions of private avarice and the tyranical policy of nations.† Under fuch circum-

* The *univerfal* diffufion of knowledge among the common people is found only in the eaftern States.
† I have heard elderly people remark, that in the early part of their lives, it never once occurred to them that it was unjuft and iniquitous to enflave Africans. It is within a few years only that the queftion has been generally difcuffed.

E

stances, the business was begun and continued, till about 40 years ago when the society of Quakers, under the auspices of the benevolent Anthony Benezet, remonstrated against the shameful traffic. From that period powerful efforts have been made by numerous societies as well as individuals, to procure the emancipation of those already reduced to slavery, and to put a stop to further importations from Africa. These efforts have been attended with great success. In some of the northern states of America, all the slaves have been set free by constitutional declarations of rights ; in almost all of them provision has been made by law to introduce a gradual abolition of the existing slavery, and the further importation is strictly prohibited. At the same time we may remark that by a late act of the British Parliament, the slave trade is to cease in the year 1796 ; and the revolution in France has already produced very important changes in that trade and in the condition of the slaves in some of the French Islands. What will be the final result of these measures and events in the West Indies, no man can predict with any degree of assurance.

With respect to the United States of America, no great difficulties or inconveniences occur in gradually abolishing slavery in all the States north of Delaware. In the 8 States north and east of Delaware, the number of slaves is comparatively small ; being to the free inhabitants in the proportion of only *one* to *forty four ;* but in the six southern States, where the slaves make nearly *one third* of the inhabitants, the liberation of them is a matter of very serious consequence.†

To give freedom at once to almost 700,000 slaves, would reduce perhaps 20,000 white families to beggary. It would impoverish the country south of Pensylvania ; all cultivation would probably cease for a time ; a famine would ensue ; and there would be extreme danger of insurrections which might deluge the country in blood and perhaps depopulate it. Such calamities would be deprecated by every benevolent man and good citizen ; and that zeal which some persons discover to effect a *total sudden abolition* of slavery in the United States, appears to be very intemperate. Indeed it is a zeal which counteracts its own purposes ; for a sudden emancipation of such a number of slaves, instead of bettering their condition would render it worse, and inevitably expose them to perish with cold and famin. Whatever have been the means and however unjustifiable the policy by which slavery has been introduced and encouraged, the evil has taken such deep root; and is so wide-

---

† Of 40. 384 Slaves in the States north of Delaware, 32,777 are in New-York and New-Jersey ; the slaves in Pensylvania Vermont and the four New-England States amounting only to 7607. The proportion of slaves to free inhabitants is,

In the States south of Pensylvania	as	1 to 2¼
In the States north of Delaware	as	1 to 44½
In New-York and New-Jersey	as	1 to 15

In the 4 New-England States, with Vermont and Pensylvania as 1 to 190 nearly.

ly spread in the southern States, that an attempt to eradicate it at a single blow would expose the whole political body to dissolution.* In these ideas I shall probably be seconded by a great proportion of thinking men throughout the United States.

It has been suggested that the country may gradually be delivered from its black inhabitants by transporting a certain number of them to Africa every year, furnished with the necessary means of subsistence. A settlement of this kind has been already begun by a colony from Great-Britain, under the superintendance of Mr. Clarkson. Indeed if colonial establishments of this kind could be effected, without great injury to the United States, humanity and philosophy would exult at the prospect of seeing the arts of civilized nations introduced into the heart of Africa. But the practicability of this plan of colonization seems to be yet problematical. It seems not yet decided by the experiments made, whether such colonies would not dwindle away by disease, and be perpetually exposed to the hostility of the surrounding natives. Indeed, it may be an important question, whether even well civilized blacks placed in the torrid zone, where little labor is requisite to procure their necessary food and clothing, would not neglect all arts and labor, beyond what are necessary to supply immediate wants, and gradually revert back to a savage state. How far a commercial intercourse with such colonies, by exciting a taste for luxuries and the love of wealth and splendor, would tend to preserve their habits of industry and prompt them to encourage arts and manufactures, we have perhaps no certain data from which we can draw even a probable conclusion.

But other objections oppose themselves to the project of African colonization. Who is to pay the expense? The master will think the loss of his slaves a sacrifice on his part sufficiently great, without furnishing them with food, utensils, and shipping for their transportation; and the slaves are not able to furnish themselves with these articles. The funds therfore must be raised by private subscriptions, or supplied by government; and these resources cannot be relied on in the present state of America. Besides it is not certain that the slaves themselves would be willing to risk such a change of situation; as most of them are born in this country and are total strangers to Africa and its inhabitants. In this case, to compel them to quit the country, and encounter the dangers of the sea, an insalubrious climate and the hostile tribes of Africa; together with the risk of starving, would be a flagrant act of injustice, inferior only to the first act of enslaving their ancestors.

The objection that the unhealthiness of the climate renders it impossible for whites to cultivate rice and indigo plantations, and therefore it is necessary to perform this business by blacks, seems to be of little weight; or at least, it cannot be of permanent duration. It is commonly supposed that the insalubrity of the air in the southern states, arises in great measure, from the stagnant waters which cover the rice and indigo plantations. These waters indeed increase

* Non minus est probanda Medicina quæ sanaret vitiosas partes Reipublicæ, quam quæ exsiccaret. Cicero Epist.

the evil ; but the principal caufe is a much more extenfive one ; the large marfhes and vaft tracts of uncleared land in the flat country. Marfhes and ftagnant waters, in which vegetable fubftances putrify and diffolve, produce peftilential exhalations ; and when a country is moftly covered with forefts, the air itfelf becomes ftagnant and does not carry off the noxious effluvia generated in low grounds. It is with the air as with water ; its purity depends on its motion. To render any flat country healthy, it muft be cleared of its forefts, and laid open on all fides to the action of the wind. It is not fufficient to open a here and there a plantation, and leave four fifths of the earth covered with wood. Befides the advantage of giving motion to the air on an extended plain, the clearing and cultivation of the earth lays it open to the fun, whofe heat warms and dries the furface, and by removing the moifture, prevents the generation of noxious exhalations. Thus whenever moft of the land in the fouthern ftates fhall be cleared, the principal caufe of epidemic difeafes will be deftroyed ; and the free circulation of air near the furface of the earth will render the putrid exhalations from the plantations and marfh ground which cannot be drained, much lefs fatal. The New-England States, fixty years ago, were infefted with the fame annual fevers, which now prove fo troublefome to the fouthern ftates ; but by the clearing and cultivation of the earth, thofe difeafes no longer prevail. The rice fields in Italy and Spain, are all cultivated by white people, and tho they render the air about them lefs falubrious than it is in other parts of the country, yet it is not fo fatal to the health of the people, as to difcourage the culture of that ufeful grain.+

There is therefore no queftion that a general and high ftate of cultivation will, to a great degree, correct the infalubrity of the low flat country in the fouthern States, fo as to render it cultivable with white laborers ; except perhaps in the vicinity of fuch faltmarfhes as cannot be drained. But the obftacles that prefent themfelves to the project of *colonization*, and to that of a *general fudden abolition* of flavery, appear to be equally infurmountable. The blacks in the fouthern States muft, it is prefumed, continue there, for a great number of years, perhaps forever ; government at leaft will not undertake the herculean tafk of exporting them to a foreign country, and repeopling five or fix States with white inhabitants.*

+ See Bourgoanne's travels, vol. 2.
* The project of exporting all the blacks in the United States, would, if practicable, be attended with many defireable effects. The feparation of the whites from all mixture of colour, would remove the caufes of much jealoufy and diffention, which will otherwife prevail among the whites and blacks. But fhould colonization ever be attempted, the exportation of the flaves from the fouthern States muft be flow and gradual, to prevent the impoverifhment of the country. The fudden expulfion of 700,000 morefcoes from Spain, in the riegn of Philip 3, gave a blow to the agriculture and manufactures of that kingdom, which the efforts of almoft two centuries have fcarcely repaired. Wat. Phil. 3, 442 Many of the welthieft people in Spain were reduced to poverty and diftrefs !—Perhaps a more eligible fcheme would be to affign the blacks a portion of land in the United States, and remove them all thither by flow degrees, furnifhing them with means of cultivation.

What then can be done? What method can be devised for meliorating the condition of the blacks, without essentially injuring the slave, the master and the public. This is the great desideratum. There appears to me only one plan or expedient for effecting this desirable object, which, in its operation, will combine the three several interests which are to be consulted; this is, to raise the slaves, by gradual means, to the condition of free tenants.

Indeed if we judge from the fate of villanage in many parts of Europe, it is no illfounded prediction, that slavery in this country will be utterly extirpated in the course of two centuries, perhaps in a much shorter period, without any extraordinary efforts to abolish it. The negroes in the southern States are very nearly in the situation of the villains in England under the first princes of the Norman line. They enjoy certain privileges, such as that of cultivating a spot of earth for themselves, on a certain day of the week, or that of performing a certain task every day. To these privileges they adhere with pertinacious obstinacy. No power or persuasion can prevail on a negro to plant or dig, in one day, more than a quarter of an acre of land; nor to labor for his master on a day which he has been accustomed to consider as his own time. The slaves will therefore relinquish no privilege; but it is scarcely possible to prevent them from gradually acquiring new privileges, which they will immediately challenge as rights, and thus by degrees abridge their masters authority over them. The humanity of some masters, the weakness or the policy of others will continually be multiplying and enlarging the privileges of their slaves, till multitudes of them acquire some property, by which they will be able to purchase more ample exemptions from their masters authority, and finally to obtain their freedom. In this manner, and by various other means, the ancient villains of England obtained their freedom, and long before the abolition of military tenures under Charles 2, there were very few villains left in the nation.* By such means, the slaves in these States would unquestionably rise to the enjoyment of freedom, without any legislative provision for the purpose. But this progress would be too slow to satisfy the friends of humanity, in this enlightened period of the world; too slow for the spirit of our governments, and too slow for our public prosperity. It is therefore highly necessary that public measures and private societies should lend their aid to accelerate the progress of freedom, and with all convenient speed, banish the galling chains of bondage from the shores of our Republic.

To the plan of raising the slaves to the condition of free tenants, many objections may be raised; but perhaps none of them will deserve an answer, except this; that if the slaves are set at liberty, even with the offer of farms on a small rent, they will not labor but will become vagabonds and starve, or betake themselves to pilfering, and be a scourge to the country. This objection has weight, and as it respects a *total* and *sudden emancipation*, it appears

---

* Black. Com. Vol. 2, 96. Sullivan, Lecture 25.

to me infuperable. But I cannot believe all the flaves in this country are fo dull that motives of interest will make no impreffion on their minds, or that they are fo unprincipled and ungrateful, that if fet at liberty, they would turn their hands againft their mafters, and devote themfelves to an idle life and to ftealing. Some among them might be found, who, if their mafters would give them farms on a moderate rent, and their liberty, on condition of their being good tenants, would be prompted to induftry, and exercife the virtues of honefty, and frugality. Every planter might find, among his flaves, a few perhaps of the young men, whofe habits are not firmly riveted, on whom the firft experiments might be made. Once infpire them with a love of property, let them go to market for themfelves, accuftom themfelves to make bargains, and begin to furnifh themfelves with clothes and food above their ordinary fare, and to build for themfelves convenient houfes, and their want continually multiplying will beget habits of induftry and economy. To prompt a flave to exertion, his defires muft be inflamed, like thofe of other men, with a profpect of enjoyments above thofe of a flave—he muft be infpired with emulation; and to fuppofe the negroes in America to be naturally deftitute of fuch defires, is contrary to hiftorical facts, and all the known principles of the human conftitution.

If a few flaves could be found on whom fuccefsful experiments might be made, the tafk would be half-accomplifhed; as example would have a powerful effect in exciting a fpirit of emulation. But to give fuccefs to any efforts for this purpofe, the flaves muft be affifted with the fuperintending care and direction of their mafters or overfeers, as well as with the ftock and utenfils neceffary for their farms. To put a man upon a farm, who has never had any will of his own, and whofe faculties, fubject to perpetual compulfion, have never had an opportunity to unfold and exert themfelves, is like fending children into the world to feek their living; and to give him land to work on, without ftock or inftruments of hufbandry, would afford a very unpromifing profpect of fuccefs.

But the firft effays would be few and on a fmall fcale, fo that the proprietor need not be terrified at the expenfe, and after the firft difficulties fhould be overcome, the tenants would be able to furnifh themfelves with the neceffary means of managing their farms, and the profits would amply repay the proprietor.

It is to be wifhed that fome patriotic and humane gentlemen in the fouthern States would make effectual experiments upon their flaves, to determine how far a project of this kind will anfwer the double purpofe of giving freedom to a miferable race of men, without injuring their owners and obftructing the cultivation of the country. No efforts of this kind have yet been made in America;* fo that our planters have not to encounter the difcouragements ari-

---

* I am informed by two very intelligent and refpectable gentlemen, the Hon. David Ramfay Efq. of South-Carolina, and the Hon. James Maddifon Efq. of Virginia, that there are no inftances of planters leafing lands to their manumitted blacks in the States where they live, as none that deferve the name of experiments.

fing from a failure of their own experiments'; and the fuccefs of fimilar attempts in Europe affords good ground of encouragement.

A glorious experiment of this kind has been made by Zamoifki, formerly great Chancellor of Poland, who in the year 1760, enfranchifed the peafants of 6 villages, in the palatinate of Mafovia. The fuccefs deferves to be particularly mentioned, as the precedent is important, and ferves to confirm the principles here advanced, that flavery is pernicious to the morals, as well as to the induftry and population of a country. On infpecting the parifh regifters of thefe villages, it appeared, that for ten years immediately preceding their enfranchifement, the births amounted to 43 each year on an average ; but in the firft ten years of their freedom, the births on an average, were 62 for each year, and in the feven following years they averaged 77. During the fame period of 17 years, the income of this particular eftate was tripled.

While the peafants were in a ftate of vaffalage, Zamoifki was obliged to build cottages and barns for them, and furnifh them with feed, ftock and implements of hufbandry. But fince they have acquired their freedom, they are able to provide all thefe neceffaries for themfelves, and pay an annual rent to the proprietor, in lieu of the perfonal fervice which was formerly exacted.

In point of morals, the improvement of the peafants is equally remarkable. While they were flaves, they were frequently guilty of grofs crimes, and fometimes in a fit of drunkennefs, would murder travellers. For fuch diforders their mafter was obliged to pay a fine, called in the polifh law, *pro incontinentia fubditorum.* Since their emancipation, fuch diforders have almoft entirely ceafed.

Upon figning the deed of enfranchifement, the benevolent Zamoifki expreffed to the peafants fome apprehenfions, that encouraged by their freedom, they would fall into every fpecious of licentioufnefs, and commit more diforders than when they were under the reftraints of a mafter's authority. The good fenfe of their anfwer is worthy of particular notice ; it was to this effect. " When we had no other property than the ftick which we hold in our hands, we had no encouragement to a right conduct ; and having nothing to lofe, we acted on all occafions in an inconfiderate manner ; but as foon as our houfes, our lands, and our cattle become our own, the fear of forfeiting them will be a conftant reftraint upon our actions." The event has manifefted the fincerity of thefe declarations, and the truth of the principles they contain. It has filenced the ill founded furmifes of the Polifh nobles, who reprefented their vaffals as too ungovernable to make a good ufe of their freedom.

Zamoifki, pleafed with the thriving ftate of his free tenants, has enfranchifed the peafants on all his eftates ; and his example has been imitated by other noblemen with fimilar fuccefs. Prince Stanislaus, nephew to the King of Poland, whofe mind has been improved by a refidence in England, warmly patronizes the plan of giving liberty to the peafants. He has enfranchifed four villages near Warfaw, and condefcends to direct and affift the peafants. He is fenfible that slavery benumbs the faculties of the mind, and renders men unfit to plan and direct the cultivation of a farm. He therefore visits their cottages, suggests improvements in husbandry, instructs them in the mode of rearing cattle and bees, and points out the errors into which they are betrayed by their ignorance and incapacity. The encreasing population and value, and the improved agriculture of the enfranchised villages, the superior neatness and convenience of the cottages, and the ease, contentment and more orderly lives of the peasants, mark most strikingly the different effects of slavery and freedom, and prove beyond cavil or controversy that the freedom of the laborer is as advantageous to the proprietor of the farm, as it is benificial to the peasant and his country.†

Why should not such illustrious examples of the happy effects of liberty upon domestic and rural economy find imitators in America? Will American planters still object to such a liberal policy, the dullness of the faculties and the inferiority of the nature, of their slaves? Will they forever be the dupes of visionary theories and a superficial philosophy? Is there no Zamoiski, no Stanislaus in the southern departments of our free Republic, who will hazard one effectual experiment? Or have false pride, deep-rooted prejudices, contempt of the African race and unconquerable indolence, such influence over the mind of our planters, that they will make no efforts to raise, from their degraded condition, the servile herd of animals, who, in the shape of men, toil like beasts of burthen, to pamper the vices of their masters, and who have as few motives to labor and as little concern for their proprietors interest or happiness, as the horse that draws his care or bears his saddle? Let Americans remember that in Poland and Russia it is yet generally believed that their peasants are incapable of obtaining any solid advantages from freedom; and that so lately as the year 1766, the economical society of Petersburgh, at the request of some unknown person, who made them a present of money for the purpose, offered a large premium, to the author of the best Dissertation on this question; " Whether it is most advantageous to the State that the peasant should possess land or only personal effects, and to what point should that property be extended for the good of the public."* To a citizen of America, it seems strange and even astonishing that in the 18th century such a question could admit of a doubt in any part of Europe; much more that it should become the subject of grave discussion. Yet not only in Russia and in great part of Poland, but in Germany and Italy, where the light of science has long since dispelled the night of Gothic ignorance, the barons would be shocked at the idea of giving freedom to their peasants.‡ This repugnance must arise from the supposition that by giving liberty to their peasants, their estates would be materially

---

† See Coxe's travels into Poland. &c. vol. 1. 159.

* One hundred and sixty-four Dissertations were sent to the Society on this occasion, and the prize was given to a Mr. Bearde, doctor in Canon and civil law at Aix-la-Chapelle. Coxe. Travels into Poland, &c. Vol. 1 p. 316

‡ Moor's Italy. p. 332.

injured ; for their *pride* alone would not withstand a regard to their *interest.* Yet this is a most fatal error, and Americans ought not to be the last to be convinced of it ; freemen not only produce more, but they squander less than slaves ; they are not only more industrious, but more provident ; and there is not an owner of slaves in Europe or America, the value of whose estate might not be doubled in a few years, by giving liberty to his slaves and assisting them in the management of their farms. For it must be remembered that slavery discourages agriculture and manufactures, not only by taking from the laborer every motive that God and Society give him to prompt him to exertion, but by inspiring the great proprietors of lands with a contempt of all manual labor, and rendering *disreputable* the very occupations from which they derive subsistence and wealth. Who could imagine that the feudal and papal systems in Europe should have so corrupted and perverted the minds of men, as to render low and degrading the noble employments of husbandry and manufactures ; employments which, in the age of Homer, were the business of kings and queens; and arts the inventors of which were deified. Astonishing truth ! The most insignificant Baron of Europe, by a customary inversion of all ideas of dignity and propriety, affects to despise the occupations over which Ceres and Minerva once presided with the rank of Goddesses. By the establishment of feuds and of the papal hierarchy, all ideas of primeval simplicity and purity of taste and manners were lost or corrupted ; kings, priests and monks engrossed all real property, and the military and sacerdotal professions alone became honorable. To so low a condition were husbandry, manufactures and commerce reduced, that in the opinion of the nobility and higher orders of the clergy throughout Europe, a nobleman could not pursue either of those occupations without degrading himself and forfeiting his rank. In a great part of Europe this opinion still prevails, and in some countries, it is supported by the laws. By a law of Poland, a nobleman is a man who possesses a freehold, or who can trace his descent from ancestors who formerly possessed a freehold estate ; who has followed no trade or commerce and is at liberty to choose the place of his habitation : but if he follows any trade or commerce, he loses his title and is degraded.* By the laws and customs of Spain, a principal proof of a man's title to nobility is, that he has never exercised any of the servile professions, and to such an extreme is this ridiculous pride and contempt of business carried in some provinces, that even merchants are not permitted to attend the theater with the nobility.†

The same prejudices still prevail in Germany;‡ the same existed in France before the late revolution, and a similar contempt of la-

---

* Coxe's Poland vol. 1. 136. 147. 149.
† Bourgoanne's Present State of Spain. vol. 2. p. 39.
‡ See Riesbeck's Travels, vol. 1. 37. 55. Preface to Born's Travels. page 14.

bor, in a greater or lefs degree, is obfervable in the Weft-Indies and in America, among the proprietors of flaves. By the prevalence of fuch falfe notions, a country is doubly injured—the proprietor and all his family are rendered unproductive hands, and moftly ufelefs—the flave or cultivator, the mechanic and the trader are rendered lefs productive and ufeful hands, by being robbed of that honorable rank and eftimation among men which is the moft powerful ftimulus to exertion, and which ought ever to be held up as a prize to reward honeft induftry. But the evil does not ftop here: Such notions render a great portion of the actual capital of a State unproductive; for when men of bufinefs have acquired fortunes, they afpire to rank, relinquifh their bufinefs, and purchafe titles. Their property, inftead of forming an active capital in trade or manufactures, is converted into real eftate or funded ftock, or what is worfe, loaned to foreigners, and the intereft confumed by this new fangled nobility, in idlenefs and diffipation. Such is the practice in many parts of Europe; and wherever this falfe pride prevails, the productive occupations of life are neglected by the wealthy and well-informed who ought to be their patrons, and who are the moft able to render them flourifhing. The confequence is, that the nobles themfelves are often poor, and their country is ftill poorer; deftitute of arts, of induftry and refources.

This contempt of bufinefs, wherever it prevails, is a moft ferious calamity, as it ftrikes at the very root of national induftry, and confequently of national wealth and power. A very little political arithmetic will fhow the magnitude of this evil, in a ftrong point of view. It muft be obferved that property, when employed in profitable undertakings, whether mercantile, agricultural or manufacturing, refembles money at compound intereft. If one hundred pounds produce fix pounds clear profit in a year, and the proprietor fquanders away the fix pounds at the end of the year, his capital ftock will never be enlarged. But if the fix pounds of profit, at the years end, are added to the original ftock, the proprietor then has one hundred and fix pounds as a capital for the fecond year. In this manner he proceeds, adding his profits to his ftock, which is an operation precifely fimilar to that of adding intereft to principal which produces compound intereft. Let it then be fuppofed that in a ftate or kingdom, there are 10,000 families of nobility or planters, who cultivate their lands by means of flaves and who do not labor themfelves. In 10,000 families, we may fuppofe about 70,000 fouls; one fourth or 17,500 adult males; and nearly the fame number or 17000 females. Suppofe every able bodied laborer to be worth 60 dollars by the year, which is the general hire of a laboring man in America; and every adult female to be worth 17 dollars a year, which is lefs than the actual value of female labor in America. The whole annual value of the labor of 17,500 men is 1,050,000 dollars; and that of 17,000 females, 289,000, dollars, in the whole, 1,339,000 dollars. But to be very moderate in my calculations, I will fuppofe the annual value of the labor of 10,000 families to be only 1,300,000 dollars; and this fum to be employed and augmented upon the principles of compound interest at 6 per cent. for one century. The result would be that a stock of 1,300,000 dollars would, in a century, produce upwards of four hundred and twenty millions of dollars. Ten thousand idle families therefore in a State, would, upon a very moderate calculation, and in one century, make that difference in the value of the products of that State.

This estimate supposes that stock will produce six per cent per ann. that no part of the stock or produce is diverted from constant employment, and that the 10,000 families will produce hands enough, if employed, to work the whole stock thro the whole period. Whatever deductions may and ought to be made in fact from the result of this calculation on account of circumstances not taken into consideration, still the process will demonstrate the immense difference in the effects of freedom and slavery, in regard to the wealth and power of a country.

But facts as well as calculations corroborate these principles. From the most accurate accounts of the exports of several nations of Europe, together with the revenues and imports, we are warranted in this conclusion, that the actual produce of a country is nearly in an exact proportion to the degree of freedom enjoyed by its inhabitants. The soil and climate of some countries are less favorable to industry than those of other countries, and the roads and convenience for navigation may make a considerable difference in the exports of different countries. But all these circumstances being equal, and the laboring people all enjoying equal freedom and encouragement, the exports of all countries would likewise be equal, as well as the internal consumption. If every man had land or materials of his own, his whole industry would be exerted in producing, and his appetites would be fully gratified in consuming his own productions; the surplus would be exported. These are true general principles as they respect nations. The exports of a country therefore are one of the principal criteria of the value of its productions. On this principle let us compare the industry of Spain and Poland with that of Great Britain and America. It will be admitted that the natural fertility of both Spain and Poland is equal, if not superior, to those of Great Britain and America, and in point of conveniences for foreign commerce, Spain is not inferior to either. The following table will exhibit the number of Inhabitants in each nation, the annual value of the exports from each in Spanish dollars, and what ought to be exported from Spain and Poland, if the inhabitants were as industrious, as those of Great Britain and America.

	Number of Inhabitants.	Annual Exports.
Great Britain and Ireland	11,000,000	66,000,000
Spain - -	11,000,000	18,000,000'
Poland - -	9,000,000	23,300,000

To be in proportion to Great-Britain,
Spain should export annually,   -   66,000,000
Poland   -   -   -   54,000,000

	Inhabitants.	Exports.
America - -	3,930,000	18,000,000

To be in proportion to America.
Spain should export,   -   -   50,000,000
Poland   -   -   -   41,000,000

This calculation must be very imperfect, because the internal consumption is not known in any of these countries. But it may be fairly presumed from the miserable condition of the laboring people in Spain and Poland, that the internal consumption of those kingdoms is by no means equal to that of Great-Britain and America, in proportion to the number of inhabitants. Free people who raise an abundance of provision, consume what they please—slaves, if they are not limited in the *quantity* of their food and cloathing, are still obliged to subsist on a few articles of coarse cheap food. It is probable therefore, if we could ascertain the value of the home productions consumed in these several countries, we should find the amount of the value of the whole produce of each country to be much more in favor of Great Britain and America, than the result of the foregoing calculation.†

† It may perhaps be enquired why, upon these principles, the exports of the United States of America, are not in proportion to those of Great-Britain; as the inhabitants of America are at least as free as those of Great-Britain. Perhaps the internal consumption in America, may partly account for this difference; but a more satisfactory answer is, that Americans almost all cultivate the earth, whereas a great proportion of the people in Great-Britain are manufactures; and it is a well known fact, that fewer laborers are required to produce a given value in manufactures from raw materials, especially with the use of machines; than to produce the same value by the culture of the earth. The manufacturers of England alone, are supposed to be upwards of 4,000,000 persons or 4-7ths of its inhabitants. The profits of trade in England, are estimated to be from 8 to 10 per cent. on their capital stock; and the profits on manufactures something higher.* Suppose them 10 per cent. and the interest of money five, the net profit is 6 per cent. which difference is immensely in favor of that manufacturing kingdom; for lands in America do not produce 4 per cent. net profit; probably not three.

But there is a farther explanation of this apparent difference. The exports of Great-Britain consist principally of manufactures; but the raw materials of the principal English manufactures, are imported from other countries; and when the articles are entered for shipment and exportation, the price of the raw materials is included with the price or value of the goods at the custom house. Thus about ½ of the wool manufactured in England, is imported from Spain—25,000 tons of iron, which is wrought into hardware, all the cotton and silk which are manufactured are imported. These articles furnish the principal value of the exported manufactures.

In America the case is different—almost all our exports consist of articles produced in the country; provisions, raw materials, &c. On these articles, there is only one advance; that upon the original labor and expense of producing them. But on the raw materials imported into Great-Britain, there are two advances—one to the nation producing them—and a second advance upon the labor and expense of manufacturing; to which may be added the freight and charges which are paid by the importer, and form a part of the first

* Smith's Wealth of Nations. Vol. 1. 9 and 10.

But it must be noted that the sum total of the whole exports of the United States is taken into the foregoing calculation, when in fact the southern States are cultivated by slaves. To show the advantages of the freedom of America in a fairer point of view, the calculation should be made upon those States where there are no slaves ; but this is impossible, as from the geographical position of the northern States, the produce of one State is exported from ports in another, and the actual exports of each separate State cannot be ascertained. Thus from the returns made to the Secretary of the Treasury, according to his printed report in 1791, the exports of New-York appear to be 2,516,000 dollars, and those of Conticut only 710,340 :* Whereas a considerable part of the ar. exported from New-York are the produce of Connecticut. A n. exact rule for ascertaining the real produce of a State is to devide

cost to the manufacturer, and on which likewise he has an advance. Suppose the fine wool imported into Great-Britain from Spain, to be worth, in the fleece, 1/6 sterling a pound ; at this price, 40,000 cwt. which is about the quantity annually sent to Great-Britain, will amount to 300,000l. Suppose this wool at the place of shipment to be worth 20 per cent. more, the value of this article to Spain may be estimated at 360,000. Suppose the freight and charges to be 5 per cent ; this wool will cost the importer 390,000l.—and if the importer is not the manufacturer, the former must also have his advance upon the wool ; so that the manufacturer will probably pay 420,000l. for this quantity of wool. He then works the wool into cloth ; but in the process, it goes through several hands, who all have a profit on their labour ; and finally the articles manufactured are exported, with an advance or profit of 10 or 12 per cent. on the original value in the fleece, and on all the intermediate advances. To these circumstances, it is probably owing that the exports of Great-Britain, exceed in value those of America, in proportion to her inhabitants ; and not to any superior industry of the nation. Perhaps also the minerals, tin and lead, may furnish a greater value with a given portion of labor, than land. On this I am not qualified to decide ; but England exports in these articles, about 2½ millions sterling annually. America exports no mineral productions worth notice. It is probable however, that the lands in England, produce more than in many parts of America, where the same labor is bestowed upon both. The high state agricultural improvements in that country, warrants this conclusion. America was a wilderness 170 years ago ; the whole country was covered with one immense forest. The land was to be cleared of enormous trees—fences were to be made—roads opened—bridges built—houses and barns to be erected, before a surplus of labor could be applied to produce articles for exportation. New settlements struggle many years with these difficulties, before they can procure a comfortable subsistence and accommodations, and a considerable part of our inhabitants are yet in this situation. Lands in England, are lately rented at 20s. sterling an acre ; but I believe but little or none can be found in America, except for gardens, worth half the money. But whatever may be the productiveness of Great-Britain, the enormous duties and taxes paid by the people, counterbalance the benefits proceeding from their industry. All the yearly taxes, and public contributions in Connecticut, including duties on imports and all other charges, are considerably less than 2 dollars for every soul. But the public contributions of all kinds in Great-Britain, amount to ten dollars a soul. That is in Great-Britain, one fourth of the annual subsistence of the people, is paid in duties, tithes and taxes—in America, the public receives of each person, only one eighteenth of his subsistence.

* The value of the exports of Connecticut is 1,150,000 dollars a year, or something more.

whole value of the exports from the United States, by the number of Inhabitants in that State.—And a ftill more accurate rule is to feparate the northern from the fouthern States, and divide the value of the exports from the northern ftates, by the inhabitants in any one northern State. Drawing a line between Pennfylvania and Delaware, which may be properly called the line between the freedom and the flavery of the cultivators in the United States, we may afcertain, upon the foregoing principles, the real value of the exports of each State.† The following ftatement will exhibit the difference between freedom and flavery in the United States.

Number of Inhabitants in the United States and
  Vermont in 1791, inclufive of Weftern Territory, fuppofed 35,000—(in round numbers)   3,928,000
Number of Inhabitants fouth of Pennfylvania, *exclufive* of Weftern Territory,   -   1,925,000
Number of ditto north of Delaware,   -   1,967,000

                                                        Dollars.
Annual value of Exports, fouth of Pennfylvania,   8,326,000
Value of Exports, north of Delaware,   -   9,245,000
Difference in number of Inhabitants in favor of the
  northern diftrict.   -   -   -   42,000
Difference in value of Exports in favor of the nor-
  thern diftrict,   -   -   -   918,000
Surplus of Exports in the northern diftrict, beyond
  the proportion of Inhabitants,   -   -   721,000

By this ftatement it appears that the fouthern ftates, which are cultivated moftly by flaves, tho fome of their principal articles of produce rice, indigo and tobacco, are much more profitable than the produce of the northern States, do not furnifh the fame value for exportation, as the northern by the difference of 918,000 dollars annually, nor in   portion to their inhabitants, by the difference of 721,000 de   s.

The following ftatement will fhow more diftinctly the difference in the productivenefs of countries cultivated by freemen and flaves.

	Dol.	Cents.
Annual exports of Spain, to each foul	1.	62
To each family of 6½ fouls,	10.	53
Annual exports of Poland, to each foul.	2.	56
To each family of 6½ fouls,-	16.	64
Annual exports of the United States to each foul,	4.	58
To each family of 6½ fouls,	29.	77

---

† This will not fhew the advantages of freedom in the ftrongeft point of view; for in that part of America north of Delaware there are 40,000 flaves, moft of which are in New-York and New-Jerfey. But it is impoffible at prefent to be more accurate. It muft be remarked likewife that we cannot any where draw a line which will feperate the exports of one State from thofe of another; that which is here drawn may be as juft as any. Pennfylvania exports a confiderable portion of the produce of Delaware; but it is probable a greater portion of the produce of Pennfylvania is fhipped at Baltimore in Maryland. Small numbers are thrown away, as of no account in this calculation.

Annual exports of the States *South* of Penfylvania
to each foul, - - 4. 33
To each family of 6¼ fouls, - 28. 14
Annual exports of the States *north* of Delaware,
to each foul, - - 4. 70
To each family of 6¼ fouls, - - 30. 55
Annual exports of Great Britain and Ireland,
to each foul, - - 6.
To each family of 6¼ fouls, - - 39.*

Similar calculations may be made with refpect to many other countries, and the refult in every inftance, will be demonftrative of the happy effects of freedom. The moft luxuriant foil and the moft falubrious climate are advantages, which, in no country, counterballance the tendency of flavery, feudal and domeftic, to weaken and impoverifh a country.

Slavery is equally hoftile to population, as to national induftry and enterprize. A country parcelled out into large eftates is always thinly fettled, unlefs it has fome peculiar natural advantages, or abounds with manufacturers or merchants. Even under the rigors of the feudal tyranny, Germany and Italy, by engroffing the

---

* In the printed report of the Secretary of the Treafury in 1791, from which the value of exports here ufed is taken, there is mentioned a deficiency in the returns from South-Carolina and fome fmall ports. This will make a fmall difference in favor of the fouthern ftates. At the fame time it is prefumed this circumftance is ballanced by the produce of Pennfylvania exported from Maryland and Virginia. Maryland contains only *one fixth* of the inhabitants, fouth of Pennfylvania, yet its exports amount to *one fourth* of the whole exports fouth of that ftate, which circumftance cannot be accounted for, by the greater fertility of its foil or induftry of its inhabitants. Indeed it is well known, that moft of the produce of the ftate of Pennfylvania, from the Sufquehanna weftward, is tranfported fouthward to Baltimore and the Potomak, and there fhipped for foreign markets. But fhould it be found that the exports of the fouthern ftates equal thofe of the northern, it would not be furprifing, confidering the fuperior profitablenefs of the principal articles raifed for exportation in the fouthern ftates. There are no confiderable articles in the northern ftates, which afford a profit, at all times, equal to that of rice, indigo and tobacco, efpecially the two former. Befides, other circumftances are neceffary to form the bafis of a juft calculation on this fubject—fuch are the expenfe of fubfiftence or internal confumption of home produce, the value of the imports, the balance of trade, the expenfes of each ftate in maintaining civil government, the clergy, fchools, roads, &c. I have not materials for even a tolerable eftimate of this comprehenfive kind. But it is certain the expenfes of fome of the northern ftates are beyond comparifon greater than thofe of the fouthern. I find the expenfe of maintaining the clergy in Virginia to be eftimated by Mr. Jefferfon in his notes, at 25,000 dollars a year. Suppofe it 30,000. The expenfe of the clergy in Connecticut, who are fupported moftly by taxes on their parifhes, is about 65,000 dollars a year. Virginia contains 747,000 inhabitants—Connecticut 238,000, or lefs than a third of the number—the expenfe of the clergy therefore in Connecticut to that in Virginia, is very little lefs than *feven to one*. The expenfe of fchools likewife in the eaftern ftates, will be found to exceed that of the fouthern, nearly in the fame proportion. Many other articles of public expenfe are higher in the northern ftates. But there is a moft important difference ftill to be remarked, between the northern and fouthern ftates. The ftaple articles of export from the fouthern, are rice, indigo and tobacco. To thefe

48

trade of Europe, were confiderably populous. But France and Pruffia did not fhake off the fetters of that fyftem till within the prefent century ; and Spain, Portugal, Bohemia, Hungary, Poland and Ruffia, fhow, by their poverty and fparfe population, that thofe countries are ftill held in chains. England vindicated her rights at an earlier period, and has become proportionably richer.

Facts of this kind can be neither evaded, nor contradicted ; their evidence is conclufive and irrefiftable ; they demonftrate the doctrine before advanced, that " flavery in all its forms and degrees, is repugnant to the private intereft and public happinefs of man." Let our efforts then be united to devife the moft eafy and effectual mode of gradually abolifhing flavery in this country. The induftry the commerce and the moral character of the United States will be immenfely benefited by the change—Juftice and humanity require it—Chriftianity *commands* it. Let every benevolent heart rejoice at the progrefs already made in reftraining the nefarious bufinefs of enflaving men, and pray for the glorious period when the laft flave who fighs for freedom fhall be reftored to the poffeffion of that ineftimable right.

may be added the wheat of Maryland and Virginia, the tar and turpentine of N. Carolina, the cotton of S. Carolinaa nd Georgia and the lumber of all. Of thefe articles the moft valuable furnifh a very fmall part of the immediate confumption of the inhabitants. Almoft all the rice, indigo, tobacco, tar, turpentine, and a great portion of the cotton, which are produced in thofe ftates, are exported. So many hands are employed in cultivating thefe articles, that there are not mechanics and manufacturers fufficient to furnifh the inhabitants with the neceffary utenfils and clothing. A large portion of the houfehold furniture, the farming utenfils, carriages, &c. of the fouthern ftates, are *imported*—whereas thefe articles are manufactured in the northern ftates and even *exported*. A great part of the clothing of the flaves is imported into the fouthern ftates—whereas the northern laboring people manufacture almoft all their coarfe clothing. The fouthern ftates alfo import feveral articles of provifion, as cheefe ; fome of them import beef and pork, all which are *exported* from the northern to a confiderable amount; not to mention wines and other liquors, of which the fouthern ftates require a larger fupply than the northern. It is probable therefore, that a much *greater proportion* of the actual *produce* of the fouthern ftates is *exported*, than of the northern; becaufe a *fmaller proportion* is confumed by the inhabitants. This will very much reduce the value of the real products of the fouthern ftates. For example, fuppofe the northern ftates to export the value of 10 millions annually, and to confume of their own productions the value of 70 millions, which is about the actual confumption, they then import the value of 10 millions in money or goods, and the whole produce is 80 millions. Suppofe the fouthern ftates to export alfo the value of 10 millions, and to confume of their own productions only 65 millions value, the *whole produce then is only 75 millions*. This ftatement is probably fupported by facts ; and there is no queftion that with all the advantages of foils, fitted to produce the moft profitable articles of commerce in the vegetable kingdom, except the fugar cane, the fouthern ftates produce much lefs in proportion to their population than the northern. Indeed when we take into confideration the great numbers of idle and unproductive hands in the fouthern ftates, we fhall not be furprifed at the fact. The family that cultivates by flaves is unproductive itfelf and all its domeftics. The number of fuch families I do not know—but if there are in the five fouthern ftates, only 10,000, fuch families of fouls each, and each family has its menial fervants, there are 120,000 unproductive perfons, who add no value to the property of the ftate, but all fubfift by the labor of others. Of this

P. S. I am lately informed by an intelligent gentleman from Virginia, that many planters on the eastern fhore in Virginia have, within a few years, liberated their flaves and employed them as hired men ; and that fuch freed men are more profitable as hired men, than they were as flaves. I rely on this information and communicate it with pleafure, as it confirms what has been here advanced ; and this fuccefs will accelerate a general emancipation of flaves in the United States—an event devoutly to be wifhed.

---

number of fouls, ½ or ⅓ are adults, capable of labor ; the annual labor of 60,000 perfons, half male and half female, would, in the northern ftates, amount to 2,910,000 dollars, or nearly ⅓ of all their prefent exports. Befides, the effect of flavery upon the whites is not merely negative ; it renders them not only unproductive, but pofitively *prodigal.* Idle people are almoft always profufe and diffipated.

This view of the fubject leads to the reafons why the fonthern ftates are fo deeply involved in debt, why they have lefs enterprize than their northern brethren, and are conftantly dependant on other nations and ftates, for fome of the neceffary articles of common ufe, the materials for which are in their forefts and at their doors.

Thefe obfervations apply equally well to all the countries of Europe, where the feudal rights remain. A numerous body of nobles, with their hofts of dependants, with armies of priefts, monks and other idlers, form a long catalogue of unproductive hands and prodigals, who feed upon or wafte the produce of the peafant. They will not labor themfelves, and they deprive the peafants of all motives to labor—the confequence is natural and neceffary, their countries are poor, beggarly and defencelefs.

APPENDIX--No. I.

An Eftimate of the value of property in Connecticut---in dollars at 4/6 fterling.

	Dollars.
Land, 2,950,000 acres, varying in value from 100 dollars to 3 dollars an acre—a moderate eftimate is 8 dollars an acre for the whole,	23,600,000
There are in Connecticut 238,000 inhabitants, which number divided by 6½, the average number of fouls in a family, the quotient is, in round numbers, 36,000, which is the number of families in the State. Suppofe every 12th houfe to contain two families, and the number of houfes will be about 33,000, which may be worth on an average 170 dollars each.	5,610,000
The number of Barns muft be lefs, as in a few towns on the eaftern and fouthern part of the State, barns are not much ufed. Suppofe 25,000 at 40 dollars,	1,000,000
Houfehold furniture, and utenfils for farmers and mechanics, 150 dollars in value to each family,	5,400,000
Stock of cattle, horfes, fheep, hogs, mules and poultry 100 dollars in value to each family,	3,600,000
Churches 200 at 1200 dollars,	0,240,000
School Houfes 1000 at 20 dollars,	0,020,000
Shops, Stores and Warehoufes for merchants and mechanics—1000 at 100 dollars,	0,100,000
Mills of all kinds, forges and furnaces, 500 at 300 dollars each,	0,150,000
Court-Houfes, Jails and Workhoufes,	0,050,000
Money in funds, Specie, &c.	1,000,000
Shipping, 27,000 tons a 15 dollars,	0,405,000
Goods on hand,	1,500,000
Total,	42,675,000

Deduct 675.000 dollars for debts due abroad and for the fake of round numbers, and the whole property, real and perfonal, of the State of Connecticut, may be valued at 42 millions of dollars. This fum divided by 36,000, the number of families in the State, gives 1166 dollars, or £350 lawful money of Connecticut for the value of property belonging to each family.

No. II.

To difplay the effects of induftry among a free people, who with few exceptions labor folely for *themfelves* and not for landlords nor mafters, the following eftimate of the *annual* expenditures of Connecticut is exhibited.

	Dollars.
Civil Government, about	15,000

1000 Public Winter Schools, fly kept by men who labor in fummer. Thefe fchools are ufually

kept four months in winter.—Hire of mafters at
40 dollars, - - - - 40,000
Wood 12 Cords each fchool at one Dollar, - 12,000
Summer Schools, 1000, kept by young women for
fmall children, at 12 dollars, - - 12,000
Books, Stationary, &c. for 45,000 children, at 25
cents annually, - - - 11,250
Clergy, 200 at 300 dollars each, including falary,
wood and parochial expences, - - 60,000
50 Vacant churches, hire of occafional preaching,
eftimated, at 100 dollars each, - - 5,000
Repair of high ways, eftimated at 2d. on the pound
on the Grand Lift—about, - - 40,000
Poor, about 100 dollars to each town, - 10,000
Expenfe of 10,000 Newfpapers circulated weekly,
numerous parifh libraries and other articles not
fpecified—fay, - - - 10,000
_____
Total of Public Contributions, 225,250
Subfiftence, including repairs of utenfils and buildings, phyficians bills, &c. eftimated a 35 dollars
a head, - - - - 8,330,000
_____
Total, 8,555,250

REMARKS.

From thefe eftimates, which are founded on the beft documents
and moft judicious opinions that I have been able to obtain, it appears that the total of public contributions in Connecticut arifing
under the laws of the State (including the expenfe of books and
ftationary for fchools, which can hardly be confidered as *publi.
expenditure*) is only 94 cents to each foul, or *fix* dollars and *eleven
cents* to each family of 6½ fouls.

It appears alfo that all public contributions under the *laws of the
State* are very little more than *one fortieth* part of the annual
produce. To thefe muft be added the duties of impoft and excife
paid to the *national* government, which amount to about *one dollar* a
head throughout the United States. Each family then pays annually to the State and General governments 12 dollars 61 cents,
which, on an eftate of 1166 dollars, the average value of eftates in
Connecticut, is a little more than *one per cent* ; or *one twentieth*
of the annual produce.

If to the foregoing amount of expenditures in Connecticut, we
add half a million of dollars for the annual net profit of the labor of
the State, we fhall have fomething more than *nine millions* of dollars for the *annual value* of the *productive labor* of the inhabitants.
This is more than a *fifth part* of the value of the property, real
and perfonal, of the whole State. The refult is, that the whole
value of the real and perfonal property is reproduced in lefs than
five years.

The real eftate of Connecticut is ftated above at 30,770,000 dollars; to which add the stock of the farms, 3,600,000, and for the value of utensils of all kinds, 630,000 and the total amount is 35,000,000 dollars. The exports of the State, being principally the produce of the earth, amount to about 1,150,000 or probably something more. The annual exports then amount to a fraction more than 3 per cent of the value of the real estates, stock, of the farms and utensils; and nearly to $2\frac{1}{4}$ per cent of the whole property of the State.

If the value of the whole annual produce of the State is nine millions, and the exports 1,150,000, the exports are a little more than $\frac{1}{8}$ of the whole produce; the other *seven parts* of the eight remain for home consumption.

No. III.

It has been shown that the Inhabitants of Connecticut contribute less than two dollars a head for all public purposes. Let this fact be compared with the state of taxes in Great Britain.

The annual revenue of Great Britain is £16,000,000 sterling or nearly 71,000,000 dollars.

Taxes for the support of the poor £2,000,000 sterling or nearly 8,888,000 dollars.

The tithes nearly £3,000,000 sterling or 13,332,000 dollars.

　　　　　　　　　　Total 93,220,000 dollars.

Other public contributions are not known and omitted.

This sum divided among the inhabitants of Great Britain (Ireland is not included) who are estimated at 8,500,000, gives 10 dollars 95 cents to each person, and 65 dollars, 70 cents to a family of six souls.———

This is within a small fraction, six times as much as is paid in Connecticut, where public charges are probably as high as in any State in the Union. If many other public charges in Great Britain are added the calculation will be nearer the truth, and much more in favor of our own country.

The expense of subsistence in Great Britain is there estimated at *six pence* sterling a day for each person, including all descriptions of people—This amounts to 40 dollars in a year. More than a *fourth part* of this sum is paid to Government, to the clergy and the poor; whereas in Connecticut the public contributions amount only to 1-18th of the subsistence of each person, estimated at 35 dollars.

No. IV.

OF PRODUCTIVE LABORERS.

That state of society and that form of government that render the greatest proportion of the inhabitants *productive* laborers, are best calculated to make a nation prosperous, wealthy and powerful; and *e converso*, the greater number of *unproductive* hands among the people, the poorer and more feeble will they be *as a nation*, tho individuals may possess immense property.

Those men whose labor adds to the value of property already existing, or produces new and further supplies of commodities, are *productive laborers*, as *husbandmen* and *mechanics*. Those men whose labor or services add nothing to the *quantity* or *value* of property, are *unproductive*, as clergymen, lawyers, phyſicians, ſchoolmaſters, officers, ſtudents of college, domeſtic ſervants, &c. Merchants, by exporting ſuperfluous commodities, for thoſe which are more uſeful, may be ranked among *productive laborers*.

From a ſurvey of the inhabitants of Connecticut, it is preſumed there are not 4000 *unproductive* adults among the whole number of 238,000 ; which is about 1 to 60.

I know not the whole number of familes in the five ſouthern ſtates in America that poſſeſs ſlaves ; but ſuppoſe 10,000 ſuch families, which is probably a moderate ſuppoſition. In each of theſe families may be 6 whites and 6 black menial ſervants, all of whom are *unproductive*. Of theſe 12 ſouls in a family, 4 may be children incapable of much labor ; there will then remain 8 adults to a family, or 80,000 unproductive adults in the 10,000 families. If we then ſuppoſe all the other unproductive adults in thoſe ſtates to be 20,000, the whole number will be 100,000, which is nearly 1 to 18 of all the inhabitants of thoſe *five* ſtates. This circumſtance alone would make an immenſe difference between the productive labor of thoſe ſtates, and that of the northern. And this is one principal cauſe of the poverty of the feudal and Roman Catholic countries in Europe. Princes and nobility, with all their retainers and dependants, together with the *regular* clergy and an undue proportion of the *ſecular*, are all *unproductive*. One certain pernicious effect of ſlavery, then is to fill a country with an undue proportion of unproductive people ; for the maſter and all his family become idlers. Not only ſo, but in America at leaſt, it is a further diſcouragement to induſtry, by preventing the introduction of *free* laborers ; few freemen being willing to labor with ſlaves.

The hire or net profit of a free laboring man in New-England, is 60 dollars a year. The hire of a ſlave in Virginia, is only 40 dollars, even on a tobacco plantation ; yet tobacco is a more profitable article, than the produce of New-England. This circumſtance ſhows the ſtriking difference in the value of the labor of freemen in New-England and ſlaves in Virginia. The ſame difference exiſts in Virginia, for a free white cannot be hired for a year at leſs than 60 or 70 dollars.*

The average expenſe of feeding and clothing male laboring ſlaves in Virginia, is 18 dollars a year, which added to his hire, makes the annual value of his labor 58 dollars. But a laboring man in New-England, at the loweſt value of the proviſion and clothing, conſumed by people of that deſcription, cannot be maintained for leſs than 50 or 60 dollars a year. The whole value of the labor of a free white in New England, is therefore at leaſt 110 dollars a year.† This is upon an allowance of half a dollar a week or very

* Letter from the Hon. Mr. Maddiſon.
† To aſcertain the exact value of the labor of a hired man, his clothing muſt be deducted from the foregoing ſum—a hired man is furniſhed by his employer with *food* and *lodging*, but he furniſhes his own *clothing* out of his wages. Deduct 20 or rather 25 dollars for clothing, and the actual profit of a laboring man in New-England, is 85 or 90 dollars a year. The ſame deduction muſt be made for the clothing of a ſlave, hired in the ſame manner.

little more for the boarding of a man, which is too low. It is presumed the diet of every family in New-England, including men, women and children, rises nearly to half a dollar a head. Estimating the board and lodging of a male laborer at 5-6ths of a dollar by the week, which may be safely done, and his hire at 60 dollars a year, and his labor is worth 103 dollars and a third, which is nearer the truth.

When we take into consideration, the first purchase of a stock of slaves, the risk of their life and health, the expenses of subsistence and overseers, with the loss of property by their negligence and thievishness, we shall find this much the most expensive mode of cultivation. A few articles only, as rice, indigo, cotton and the sugar cane, will bear the expenses. But when we add the extravagance and profligacy occasioned among the proprietors by this mode of cultivation, all calculation must cease.

I have said in the foregoing essay, that it is probable the internal consumption of produce in the southern states, is much less than in the eastern and northern.

The estimated annual charge of supporting a male laboring slave in Virginia, is 18 dollars. The expense of supporting children must be much less—but I will include children, and suppose 18 dollars a head to be the annual charge of subsistence and clothing. Virginia contains 292,000 slaves, who, at 18 dollars each, consume the value of 5,256000 dollars. But the charge of maintenance in Connecticut (in other northern states it is nearly the same) is estimated at 35 dollars a soul. Then 292,000 free persons in the northern states annually consume property to the amount of 10,220,000 dollars. This difference of expence or internal consumption being 4,964,000 dollars, on less than 300,000 souls, shows the difference between the products of the northern and southern states ; for it is not supposeable that amount of the difference is consumed upon the luxuries of a few planters. The expence of maintenance in S. Carolina is much higher, because of the higher prices of provision and clothing ; at the same time, the culture of the rice and indigo is much more profitable. The annual exports of the southern states are less than those of the northern, in proportion to the number of inhabitants, by the difference of 720,000 dollars. But taking into consideration the immense difference in the expense of maintaining slaves, which makes the difference of internal consumption, and there is little doubt that the actual yearly produce of the southern states, in proportion to the number of souls, is less than that of the northern by the difference of 5, 6 or 7 millions of dollars.

No. V.

Comparative view of the productiveness of Ireland and Connecticut.

Ireland contains about 3,000,000 people. Its exports amount annually to 3,500,000 sterling or 15,540,000 dollars. Its exports then equal, or rather exceed those of America, in proportion to its inhabitants. But this will not prove the superior productiveness of Ireland, for the home consumption is a material consideration.

There are in Ireland, according to Arthur Young Efq. who has examined this fubject with minute attention, about 2 million of *Cottars* (cottagers) or peafants, who moftly live on potatoes and butter-milk. They confume annually 60 barrels of potatoes in a family of 6 or 7 perfons—a barrel weighing 280lb. and containing about 4 Englifh bufhels—A barrel, at an average price throughout the country, is worth 2/7½ fterling ; or 3/6 lawful money of New-England. Then 60 barrels at 3/6—10l. 10s. or 35 dollars, which is the principal expenfe of food for a family.

The cloathing of the Irifh Cottars is trifling, the children are almoft naked great part of the year—and adults are often without fhoes and ftockings—fuppofe the clothing and additional food of a family to be 45 dollars a year, then 80 dollars is the amount of the fubfiftence of a family of 6½ fouls —which is nearly 12 1-3 dollars a head—Suppofe it 14 dollars a head then the annual fubfiftence of 2 millions amounts to 28,000,000.

That this eftimate is near the truth is evident from the price of labor in Ireland ; which, for a male laborer, amounts, on an average thro the year, to fix pence halfpenny fterling a day—Deducting Sundays and three holidays only, there remain 310 days for labor. Suppofe every man to labor 310 days in the year ; the amount of wages of a day-labourer at 6½ fterling is 1. 8. 6s. 11d. or 38 dollars nearly. In two families of 6½ fouls each or 13 perfons, there will be found 3 male adults—3 female do. 4 young perfons under adult years and 3 children.

3 Male adults at 38 dollars a year -	114 dollars.
3 Females do. at 15 do. - - -	45
4 Young perfons, whofe labor may be worth on an average 8 dollars each - - -	32
3 Children incapable of labor	

13 Perfons, total value of their labor, - 191 dollars.

Then 13..191::2,000.000 : 29,384,615 dollars, the value of the labor of 2 millions of the peafantry in Ireland.—Suppofe them to confume the whole, and call the whole, for the fake of round numbers 30 millions—Then add 20 millions more for the value of the labor of the manufacturing part of the kingdom, &c. (which is much more than the real value) and we have 50 millions of dollars for the annual value of the labor of Ireland, and the confumption of its 3 millions of inhabitants, which will be the full amount of its products. But the produce and confumption of 3 millions of people in the United States according to the rate of confumption in Connecticut, would be 105 millions. This calculation, it is prefumed, is very favorable to Ireland, and corroborates, in a ftriking degree, the doctrine I have advanced of the fuperior productivenefs of the labor of freemen who work for their own benefit.

Manner *of* Living *in* Connecticut,

'The laboring people eat and drink whatever they pleafe. Their ordinary and conftant food confifts of pork, beaf, veal, mutton, poultry (they ufually eat meat at every meal—but always twice a day) milk, bread, fometimes of pure wheat, but more commonly of wheat and rye, or rye and indian corn mixed together; butter and cheefe, potatoes and other vegetables. The common laboring people, worth from 500 to 1000 dollars are as fully fupplied with thefe articles, as the richeft nobleman in Europe. They alfo confume large quantities of tea, fugar, coffee, molaffes, and other foreign articles. Their drink is principally cider; but much rum is alfo confumed. Their cloathing confifts of coarfe woollen and linens of their own manufacture moftly; with a finer fuit for holidays.

Let this fituation of the laboring people in Connecticut, (and all the people of the northern ftates are in nearly the fame circumftances) be contrafted with the condition of the flaves in the foutbern ftates, and of the poor in great part of Europe; and let humanity and benevolence decide, whether liberty or flavery is the moft eligible, and whether a general revolution in the governments of the old world is not a defirable event. If that nation is the happieft, which with induftry enjoys a full fupply of the comforts and conveniencies of life, then that government and thofe inftitutions which diftribute and fecure to the *greateft* number of people the *greateft* portion of thefe enjoyments, will forever be the *beft*.

www.ingramcontent.com/pod-product-compliance
Lightning Source LLC
Chambersburg PA
CBHW022038080426
42733CB00007B/881